Covering the Business Beat

808.020

ENTERED SEP 2 7 2004

Columbia College Library
600 South Michigan
Chicago, IL 60605

Covering the Business Beat

Strategies for Publishing What You Write

Stephanie Hainsfurther
Emily Esterson

Purdue University Press
West Lafayette, Indiana

Copyright 2004 by Purdue University. All rights reserved

Printed in the United States of America

Library of Congress Cataloging-in-Publication Data

Hainsfurther, Stephanie.
Covering the business beat : strategies for publishing what you write /
Stephanie Hainsfurther, Emily Esterson.
p. cm.
Includes bibliographical references and index.
ISBN 1-55753-351-2
1. Freelance journalism--Vocational guidance. 2. Journalism, Commercial.
I. Esterson, Emily, 1963- II. Title.

PN4784.F76H35 2004
808'.02'023--dc22

2004006364

Contents

For Mark, as always, my love and my friend. Because of you, everything flows—the writing, the fun, the life.

—Stephanie

For Scot, for his love, his advice, his calmness, and for taking over the morning barn chores so I could get my writing done.

—Emily

Acknowledgments

Thanks, Mark Mathis, for sharing your experiences along the publishing journey and for recommending that the editors at Purdue read our proposal.

To our interviewees who took time out of their busy days to talk with us and share their know-how with our readers. Our book wouldn't be the same without you: Claire Walter, Diane Velasco, Dawne Shand, Mary Scott, Karen Raterman, Josh Hyatt, Will McNamara, Marc Ballon, Rene Jackson, Jacquelyn Lynn, Elaine Dundon, and Tania Casselle.

Trusted friend and meticulous editor Kristen Bisson was the first to read our manuscript. The tireless and loyal Kathi Schroeder was the last to read it before it went to press. Both helped us put the polish on it. We thank them for finding the holes, the missing commas, and the spelling errors, for pointing out the problems, and for offering their encouragement along the way. Their close readings of and suggestions for this book made it so much better. And to the staff of the *New Mexico Business Weekly,* and former publisher Wythe Walker, we thank you for your patience and encouragement. A very special thank you goes to Jennifer Tyrrell, our editor at Purdue University Press, for her painstaking guidance in bringing *Covering the Business Beat* to publication.

Introduction

Trained Journalists Are Waiting to Take Your Call!

One night before dinner, Stephanie and her husband were watching the local evening news. Just before the commercial break, the station ran a brief videotaped message, asking viewers to call in with news tips. "Trained journalists are waiting to take your call!" they announced at the end of the segment.

Stephanie laughed so hard that tears ran down her face.

Her husband thought she had lost her mind. "What's wrong with you?" he asked, concerned, but amused.

"Trained journalists? *Trained* journalists?" Stephanie asked. "I'm flying by the seat of my pants here!"

In the fifteen years she has made her living as a freelance business writer, Stephanie has received no formal training. She has not been to journalism school, nor has she taken so much as a workshop or a seminar on how to write business stories. Yet she has published more than six hundred stories in local, national, and international magazines, newspapers, and journals.

The only things Stephanie has brought to the table are a genuine love of writing—the process, not the byline—a willingness to learn, a sense of reportorial balance, and some early experience in the world of business. That's all.

Emily spent the first ten years of her adult life floundering from one job to another. At one low-wage, order-processing job at a book-importing company, she volunteered to write copy for the Christmas book catalog. That ignited a long-smoldering desire to write. She received her MBA from the University of Denver, where she edited the graduate-school newsletter. She then took a job at an oil company, writing the company's internal newsletter. Along the way, she freelanced for anyone who'd pay her. She's never had a formal journalism class.

We are sharing how we started out because you have those experiences and qualities, too, and much more. You may be working, or recently have worked, in the corporate world. You have a love and a talent for writing. There are things you want to say about the industry in which you work. Or you wonder if the life of a freelance writer would better suit you. You bought this book to help you find out.

You might write part-time now, for a company newsletter or an industry trade journal, and see your byline published there on a regular basis. You might work from time to time on nonbusiness pieces, like personal essays for the church flyer orthat novel stashed away in your drawer. Whether you've seen your work in print or not, writing is a part of your life and probably always has been.

You're a writer even though you are also a corporate manager, an entrepreneur, a training facilitator, or mailroom clerk. Whatever position you hold in the company you work for (or own), you can use that position as your starting point. Why yearn to be a "trained journalist?" To get your freelance career started, start by writing about the industry you know.

Most newspaper reporters for the business section know little about their subject matter at first. They are not trained in business and have to learn from the ground up, about things like balance sheets, return on investments, accounting practices, and all of the other things you already know from being in business. Many news reporters have never worked anywhere but in a newsroom.

As a reporter, you would be no "cub." Imagine how valuable the freelance writer who is experienced in the business he or she writes about is to an editor. That writer knows the issues in the industry in question, knows who to talk to and where to look for information. As a businessperson, you come to the job of writing about your industry with firsthand experience and lots of contacts.

How to Use This Book

Covering the Business Beat is organized to help you start and build a freelance writing career that begins right now. No wishing you didn't have to work for a living so you could go off to an island and write. No waiting for the company to change its policy against tuition reimbursement for creative-writing courses. No daydreaming, wishful thinking, or other time-wasting fantasies. This book has good, solid advice you can use to write for the publications you probably read—trade journals, local business magazines and newspapers, newsletters and membership news.

All the chapters in this book have the same basic format. There is a main text that will take you through each part of starting your writing career, and useful sidebars highlight each chapter. These sidebars will give you practical tips that you can use today to get started writing and get published. They also will be handy to refer back to when you're interviewing a subject ("Twenty-Five Questions to Ask Any Business" in chapter 4), let's say, or structuring a story ("Shaping Up" in chapter 5).

In addition, we have included mini-interviews with editors of and writers for business newspapers and magazines, trade journals, company newsletters, and membership association publications. These professionals report to you from the frontlines of journalism on important topics, such as what business editors look for in a freelance writer, which types of business articles always sell, and how to break into business publications.

At the end of each chapter is a reminder box, called "To Do Today," that highlights things you can do immediately to put your writing career on fast forward, culled from the text, sidebars, and interviews.

Start Covering Your Beat Today!

We interview hundreds of businesspeople every year. Invariably, as we're winding up the question-and-answer period, someone says, "So you're a writer? I've always wanted to write for a living, but . . ."

There are a lot of "buts" that keep us from doing what we love. Most of the time, we defer the pleasure of writing to make a living, spend time with our families, and meet our responsibilities. All good reasons, no question. But this book doesn't make you choose between the industry you're in and the one you'd like to be in. Stay employed (or happily retired), start writing about the field you work in, and get published. It's simple.

To trained journalists who might have dropped in, we'd like to say that we have the greatest respect for your labors and the honors awarded you in journalism school. Some of you have made invaluable contributions to this book. You filled in the many gaps in our experience with a knowledge of business writing that could only be gained firsthand. You work for popular publications known for fairness in reporting and outstanding writing and editing. No doubt, some of you edit and write for major television newsrooms and well-known business publications.

We're not saying that being trained in journalism is unnecessary. We're just saying there is plenty of business writing out there for the rest of us to do. And that life experience in an industry, and the daily dealings within the business world, can give a business professional the know-how and material to turn a "wannabe" into a writer.

We'll help you turn that business savvy into bylines.

—Stephanie Hainsfurther and Emily Esterson

1. Network, Don't Query

Every Friday morning in Boulder, Colorado, a group of writers gathers at the Book End Café. This group, which calls itself BMWs, or Boulder Media Women, consists of freelance journalists, public-relations professionals, editors, and marketing folks. Many, if not all, are self-employed freelancers. Although there is a core group that shows up every week, the BMWs, which celebrated its tenth anniversary in May 2001, morphs frequently, adding new members as others disappear. The only limitation is the size of the café. Although the women definitely socialize, it's unabashedly a networking group. People talk about what projects they're working on and which editors in town might be hiring freelance writers for which projects.

One regular member, Claire Walter, is a ski writer. Walter once told a class of aspiring magazine writers: "My business is ski writing. I write for money. It's the best job in the world."

Walter markets herself constantly. She networks constantly. She belongs to the American Society of Journalists and Authors, the Society of American Travel Writers, North American Snow Sports Journalists Association, and the Colorado Authors' League. She attends ski-industry conferences around the country and New York City writers' conferences. When she goes to New York, she sets up appointments with editors. She has a website, where the covers of her last three books are displayed, and a link to a long list of articles.

Emily Esterson, co-author of this book, met Claire Walter at a BMWs' meeting. When Emily needed ideas for a special ski issue of a city magazine she later edited in Boston, she called Walter in Boulder. Not only did Walter have great ideas for stories, she knew two really good New England–based ski writers who could help with the issue. She also wrote one of the pieces. And although Walter still writes the occasional query letter, she says, "I hate to do it—and I don't find it especially effective."

Emily has more than one hundred articles in print. She's written one, yes, *one* successful query in her ten-year professional life as a journalist. The very first article she sold came about because she had the chutzpah (or stupidity) to cold-call an editor on the phone, introduce herself, give her nonexistent credentials, and tell him she wanted to write a story for him. Turned out he had attended the same MBA program and was willing to work with a new writer on a short piece. The assignment was four hundred words long and paid twenty cents per word. Not bad for the first time out.

Forget the Query Letter

If you've been considering becoming a writer, part time or full time, you've likely picked up a how-to book on how to break into publishing. Perhaps you've taken a continuing education class on writing for publication. Undoubtedly, you've spent some time writing the omnipresent query letter.

A query letter, for the uninitiated, is a brief business letter that outlines the main points of a potential article, gives a bit of background about the writer, and most importantly, gives an editor an idea about the query letter author's writing skills and voice. In a query letter, you have a few lines, at most, to catch an editor's attention. Aspiring freelance writers are often counseled to try writing a query letter, sometimes called a pitch letter, to sell stories. These letters require enough research for the writer to develop a strong angle.

The hard truth is that it's very rare for editors to assign stories from a query letter (unless the idea and angle are unique, and the writing is clear and error-free). The first, more effective step is to make personal contact with an editor.

In the classes Emily teaches, she goes over formal query-letter writing as an exercise only, because it can help a beginning writer to focus an idea and develop a story outline. However, she advises that the students make some kind of personal contact before they send a query. One student, who also happened to be majoring in architecture, actually took Emily's advice (a miracle!) and cold-called the managing editor of a magazine to pitch a story about a local architect. The editor told him to send an email query, and they corresponded back and forth for a few weeks about the idea. Although the student didn't actually get the assignment, he was invited to pitch again. The editor now knows his name. Making personal contact is the important thing: without that name recognition, query letters often disappear into the abyss that is an editor's desk.

Here's another reason to forget queries: they take too much time. The key to writing a successful query letter, as you may have read, is to do enough research so that you can hit the ground running if you should be so lucky as to get an assignment. Also, your query letter needs to include sources and some intelligent verbiage that shows you have some knowledge about the subject matter. This is good advice, provided you are independently wealthy and can sit around waiting for an editor to a) find your query, b) read it, and c) respond to it.

Think of it this way: As a businessperson, you don't spend a lot of time developing a product until you know there's actually a market it for it, right?

Myths and Truths about Query Letters

Myths:

1. Editors are waiting to read your queries.
2. A well-written query will always get an editor's attention.
3. You should never call an editor after you've sent a query.

Truths:

1. Editors are busy. Some get thousands of queries every month, and most of these query letters go unanswered.
2. Editors rarely make assignments from blind query letters, even if the queries are exceptionally well-written and researched.
3. If an editor asks for a written query, the query you write can be less formal. Write a headline for your article, list three or four points from the storyline, and cite your sources. Sum up with one sentence that tells why this story suits the publication and its readers. That's it.

You wouldn't manufacture a widget without first knowing what precise features widget customers want (or even if they want widgets). Writing and researching a query letter is like manufacturing a widget without a customer and his or her needs in mind. *As a freelance writer, your customer is the editor, and your product is the writing*. If you don't know the customer, how can you produce a widget he or she will want to buy?

Like gaining new customers for a business, successful freelance writers get most of their business from word-of-mouth. You can use the same networking skills you use to get the word out about your day job as you do for your freelance writing. It's very simple. Approach the job just as you would approach a business development effort at the company where you work. Good sales people join leads groups, associations in their industries, the local Rotary Club, or the local chapter of national sales organizations. They attend conferences and business luncheons and social and charity events, and while they're at it, they hand out business cards like crazy. Sometimes they cold-call potential clients with a nicely honed pitch they can deliver in a confident, succinct manner.

Using exactly the same tools, you can sell yourself as a freelance writer, and sell your product—your writing. This networking has an added benefit: you begin to build a bank of unique article ideas. Think of your time spent networking as having a dual purpose: market research for your product (articles) and sales for your business (yourself, freelance writer).

As an insurance professional, for example, you might already belong to your local insurance underwriters' or agents' group. Perhaps you also belong to the local chamber of commerce, and the American Marketing Association's local chapter. When you attend these meetings, put on your freelance writer hat and listen closely to the conversations around you. Chances are, you'll pick up article ideas left and right. Someone may be talking about the newest product his or her firm is offering, or the luncheon speaker is expounding on an important economic trend that could have an impact on the industry. What you hear could spark ideas for articles to sell to an insurance trade publication. Take notes. This is your market research, this is the expertise and insider's knowledge you can sell. As editors, we kick our reporters out of the office to send them to these meetings. Why? To gather material, to network, to meet sources, to learn about the industry they cover. The same holds true for freelancers. Get out and meet people.

Be a guest speaker or a teacher yourself. Stephanie Hainsfurther, co-author of this book, was invited to speak on a media panel at a conference for businesswomen. Also on the panel was a reporter for *New Mexico Business Weekly*, who was impressed by Stephanie's professionalism as a freelance writer. When the paper's managing editor needed a feature article in a hurry, the reporter suggested Stephanie. Four years later, Stephanie was still a regular feature writer for *New Mexico Business Weekly*.

Industry trade shows are another way to meet editors and others who might give you work. The trade publications that cater to that industry will undoubtedly have a booth in the exhibition hall. Often the editor and the reporters are working the booth or mediating a session. This is a great venue in which to meet trade publication staff because they're away from their cluttered, chaotic desks and have time for socializing. Often their mission at these trade shows is the same as yours—to meet people.

You'll also want to get to know the heads of marketing departments for local businesses, public-relations professionals, CEOs, CFOs, other freelance writers, and full-time reporters. You never know when someone will ask you, "Hey, do you know anyone who can write a company newsletter for us?"

Be a Joiner

In addition to your professional groups, join every organization that has something to do with the written word. Think of this as the business development part of the job. Although you may not be interested in writing public-relations materials, attending the local chapter meeting of Public Relations Society of America can introduce you to public-relations professionals who undoubtedly know editors and know what they are looking for.

Join the local Writers' Guild, American Society of Journalists, and any writing association that is specific to your industry. And don't just join: go to events whenever possible.

Another way to meet editors and writers is to take an adult education course in writing for publication. Often, a local journalism professional conducts such a course (which will undoubtedly include a long section on writing query letters). This will give you the opportunity to get to know the teacher, who can then guide you to other networking opportunities. Some of the other students might already be professional freelancers, or could be in the future. Other writers are great sources for writing assignments.

What to Take to a Networking Event

- ☐ Business Cards ☐ Pens ☐ Notebook ☐ Calendar

What to Bring Home

- ☐ Other people's business cards—editors, heads of marketing departments, human-resources professionals (corporate newsletters are big business for freelancers). Emily often annotates the backs of business cards: "Needs articles on depression in workplace for newsletter," or "source for insurance cost story."
- ☐ Three or four article ideas
- ☐ Notes from speeches and from conversations with people. Writers make notes about everything. You never know when some tidbit dropped in conversation will end up as an anecdote in a story.

Go Straight to the Top

Gather all the business publications that are published in your town. That would include business newspapers, specialty journals, even the local newspaper's business section. Just as if you were prospecting for new clients, cold-call the editors and ask if you can spend ten minutes with them conducting an informational interview. Tell them you'd like to learn about their business and how to break into it. Most editors are flattered to be considered the experts and are willing to share their knowledge. And, believe it or not, they are always looking for new writers.

The whole point to getting to know the editors is to help you avoid the slush pile—spending hours or days researching a blind query letter, only to have it end up in the trash can. Editors will know your name and a little something about you. When you meet with the editor, bring copies of any published clips you may have. Ask the editor what he or she likes in a story and what are the "must haves" for an article for that publication. Ask him or her which story in the newspaper was that editor's recent favorite. And don't be afraid to ask advice about breaking into the business. Remember, many editors have been in your shoes. Always follow up with a thank you, and, if you've got a pitch, this is the time to throw it. The meeting will (hopefully) have left a favorable impression on the editor, and he or she might be more willing to listen to your story pitches. When you have an idea that would suit that editor and his or her publication, simply call and say, "Thanks for the meeting, and I was wondering if you would be interested in . . ." Make it good. This may be your only opportunity.

Don't Forget the Writers

Don't limit your meet-and-greet activities to editors. Freelance writers often pass assignments off to colleagues when they become overwhelmed, or are assigned something on a topic that is not in their area of expertise. Some of our best assignments have come through other writers, and we've tossed a few in other people's directions as well. When a freelancer can't take an assignment, editors always appreciate a good referral more than a flat no, and it makes the original writer look better, too.

Use the same technique with writers as you do with editors. Comb the publications you'd like to write for, and study the bylines. Who writes about which beat? Whose style do you like the best? Who writes content you think you might be able to write? Then call those people on the phone and invite them out for coffee. Talk to them about how they put together their stories, which editors they like to work for, and why. Take notes.

Often the best networking happens in a rather impromptu way, like the BMWs' Friday morning meeting. The point is to be networked so that when those kinds of meetings happen, you'll know about them. If there is no such group in your town, you might want to start one.

A Day in the Life

Let us paint you a picture of an editor's desk, to illustrate why you should forget everything you've ever heard about query letters In one corner, the week's newspapers, magazines, and trade journals accumulate in a perilous, leaning tower, waiting to be clipped for interesting tidbits to pass on to reporters. In another corner are budgeting items, a lost calculator, and notes on next year's freelance budget. Another contains résumés of hopeful reporters, designers, and editors. There are coffee cups growing mold and a few popcorn kernels left over from last night's preproduction snacking frenzy. Yet another pile contains miscellaneous scraps of paper on which this editor has written ideas, phone messages, a

Tools to Build Your Network

If you want to keep your professional life separate from your writing life, create a business card for your writing side. You can do this on most home computers, although it may be worth it to have your cards professionally designed and printed. Keep it simple and professional; if you'd like, you can even name your business. Just make sure the name has relevance to the work you're doing. You can also just use your own name, and the words "freelance writer."

Using the same design, create some nice letterhead. Use this letterhead to send thank you notes and "FYI" notes when you come across something you think might interest an editor.

Put a professional-looking signature on your outgoing emails. Make sure the signature includes your full name, company name, address, phone/fax, and email.

It goes without saying, but always carry a pad and pen with you on your networking voyage, along with your business cards. You'd be surprised how many times we've lent fellow journalists pens or pieces of paper at networking events.

random thought or two—utter chaos. And that doesn't even include the electronic correspondence waiting in the editor's email inbox or the faxes that his or her assistant reads. And you think your query letter is going to rise up magically from those stacks of junk and catch an editor's attention? Hardly.

An editor oversees the entire content of the newspaper or magazine. Quality control, budgeting, editorial content, and public speaking all fall within the editor's job description. Newspaper and magazine editors have different modifiers before their titles, such as "managing" editor, or "assistant" editor, or "research" editor. Potential freelancers need to make an effort to find out what different titles mean at different publications, because they can vary widely. As managing editor for the business newspaper *New Mexico Business Weekly*, Emily runs the newsroom and interacts directly with freelancers, giving out assignments with her guidance and editing copy as it arrives. However, at *Inc.* magazine, the managing editor is the business manager for the magazine and has little contact with the writers. At *Inc.*, the senior editors work with the freelancers.

Different editors also might manage different sections of their publications. If you want to write a small-business profile, for example, you might deal with the small-business section editor.

Editors are extremely busy people. These chronically overworked and often harassed individuals receive piles of press releases (electronic and pulp) from legions of public-relations people. Much of what they receive has little relevance to what they do on a day-to-day basis, or to filling up the newspaper or magazine with germane and interesting content. To keep their publications strong, they also spend a good deal of time helping reporters and freelancers, serving as coaches for those less experienced and line editors for those who have the basics down pretty well. This means lots of time talking to reporters and reading copy.

An editor's time is dictated by the ebb and flow of deadlines. The editor of a weekly publication may have down time right after it goes to press, but it could only be a window of a day and a half. A monthly editor may have a week or so before the cycle begins to ramp up again. This is the time they usually spend reading all those magazines, cleaning off those piles of paper, and assigning stories. As an editor gets closer to production, more and more pressing assignments appear on his or her desk, and he or she tends to put all nonessential projects aside until the beginning of the next cycle. If you plan to call an editor on the phone, make sure you know what day the publication goes to press. Don't call the editor for two days before that day.

Instead, learn when the down days are and what an editor does on those down days. You can call the editor's assistant and ask when his or her editor is most available, or simply call the publication office and ask when the newspaper or magazine goes to press. The day after is usually a good time to call. Some editors schedule meetings and lunches, others just clean their offices and catch up on email. Always begin a phone conversation with an editor with the following sentence: "Hello [editor], this is [your name]. Is now a good time to talk?" If he or she is on deadline, he or she will tell you.

The more editors you know, the more likely you'll be to find someone who wants to work with you. Your job is to make yourself indispensable to the editor, and the more you know about his or her professional life and needs, the more likely you'll be able to deliver. Once you prove you can deliver, you become that very product that your editor just can't live without. He or she keeps buying your articles, over and over. It's that simple.

To Do Today

- ☐ Join your local writers' association.
- ☐ If you don't already belong, join a trade association in the field you'll be writing about.
- ☐ Take an editor to lunch.
- ☐ Take a writer to dinner.
- ☐ Collect local and trade publications for which you would like to write.
- ☐ Gather writer's guidelines from those publications and find out when their deadlines are.

Interview with Mary Scott,

of Denver, Colorado, former businessperson and now a successful freelance business writer.

How did you get your first assignments?

I was marketing director at the North Face in Berkeley, Calif. [an outdoor clothing and equipment retailer]. I worked with all of the editors at the trade magazines, as well as the ski and outdoor publications. The editor of the now-defunct *Outside Business* (the trade version of *Outside*) interviewed me regularly. She asked if I wanted to write a column about marketing. It turned into a monthly feature.

When I was laid off at North Face, I decided to give freelance writing a shot. I contacted all the editors I knew and got assignments, eventually writing regularly for *Powder*, *Outside*, and *Skiing*. I then sent clips of these to *USA Today* and eventually wrote a monthly article on participatory sports. I also wrote a weekly participatory-sports story for the *Marin Independent Journal*.

It was about that time that I met Howard Rothman. He and I were both contributing writers to *Outside* and *Outside Business* magazines. We met at trade shows and became friends. We co-authored a book, *Companies with a Conscience*. That led me to become a contributing writer for *Business Ethics* magazine; they had run an excerpt of the book, so I called them and asked for assignments, which they gave me. When their editor left, I became the editor of *Business Ethics*. The publisher folded the magazine after one year; I then got a full-time job working at New Hope Communications as a trade-magazine section editor in the natural products industry.

That industry went through a major downsizing, so I again lost my job after two years. Luckily, I had already started pursuing freelance opportunities and for the past two years have been freelance writing full-time. Now, two years later, I am making double the salary as when I worked a full-time job.

How did you keep moving on to other assignments?

I knew as an editor that it was difficult to find good financial writers. When you did, they commanded high rates. So that's where I decided to focus my efforts.

I started writing the book column for *Research*. My editor there recommended me to the editor of a sister publication, *Buyside*. And I actually found the *Frontline* job [a financial publishing company] in mid-2000 through the Internet (I advertised on www.sunoasis.com). And now I am writing a new version of *Companies with a Conscience*.

It seems like you really know how to network. How do you go about soliciting new work from editors, especially outside of Denver, where you live and work now?

Everyone I work for is in California. I have never met, in person, my editors at *Buyside* or *Research*. *Frontline* hosts meetings twice a year for its freelancers, so I've met the management and staff there.

If I *were* to solicit new work, I would contact everyone I know personally—other writers, former colleagues, you name it—and ask for ideas. As any editor will tell you, it's hard to find good, reliable writers. So if a person has the skill and is efficient, an editor would be thrilled to find him or her.

Start with what you know best. Contact the editors of the niche publications/trade magazines that cover the industry you work in. Consider the local weekly newspaper. The first goal is to get clips. From there, you can send those clips to larger, more mainstream publications.◆

2. What the Market Will Bear

Through your networking activities, you now have an idea of the publications in your town. But you need to know much more: which of these publications might be interested in your work, what other publications might be suitable for you, and what types of articles do they all want to buy.

Your writing is your product. Just as you would if you were launching a new product, you must design your writing product to meet the needs of each potential customer.

Let us look for a moment at the market for calculators: If we produce a nice simple calculator, the market includes countless types of people, right? Students may buy it, executives may buy it, senior citizens may buy it. If we make the keys bigger, eliminate a few of the more complex functions, enlarge the number display, then maybe we're shooting directly for the senior-citizen or the elementary-student market. If we shrink it to pocket size, it fits well in an executive's briefcase. If we add a bunch of functions, it sells to university students studying science and mathematics.

The same is true for your writing. The work you do on a company marketing newsletter can be repackaged into a trade-magazine article. The how-to article you write for a trade magazine can be broadened to sell to a consumer magazine. A tweak here, a tweak there, and you can sell it to various markets. But you need to know what you're writing, why you're writing it, and who will read it.

Study the Markets

In the previous chapter, we asked you to gather all of the local and trade publications in your industry for which you may want to write. To finish compiling your "potential markets" library, head off to one of those bookstores or newsstands with aisles of both popular and obscure magazines and newspapers. These are the best places to begin your research. You can see a variety of magazines, organized by category. Look through them to get a feel for the quality of the photography, graphics, and paper. Often a writer can learn a lot about a publication just from looking at the layout. If it's printed on thin, flimsy paper, the publication may be trying to save money. If the magazine is particularly fat and full of sophisticated advertisements, it may be doing quite well. Design can also tell you about tone. If it has little art and a straightforward design, the editors might prefer a more serious tone.

There are many more potential markets than just the magazines that you'd find at newsstands. Trade and membership associations in your industry can provide you with a list of leading publications.

Many general-interest and other magazines carry business-oriented stories that you may be able to write, using your specialized knowledge. *Better Homes and Gardens* frequently runs articles about home finance. *Natural Home* carries an article about energy in each issue.

Once you get your magazines home, spread your favorites on a table. Most magazines or other publications have a statement of purpose. You'll often find this mission statement in the *Writer's Market* listing for that publication (see "Suggested Reading," p. 125), or on the *masthead* of the publication, the strip alongside the page, usually in the front of a magazine, which lists the publication's staff. Examples include "*Home Energy:* We provide practical information for professionals in residential energy conservation and home performance" or "*Home Furnishings Executive:* We hope that home-furnishings professionals view our magazine as a profitability tool. We want each issue to help them make or save money." As you can see, the magazine business defines niche marketing—every publication has a specific reader in mind.

At this point, begin to write your observations down on a sheet of paper. In effect, you'll be making a "story map" of the magazine, which will come in handy when you pitch your ideas to the editor.

Look again at the publication's masthead. Learn the names of its staff, then page through the publication and count the number of articles by each person, and the number of articles written by people not listed there. Count the *contributing editors* and *writers* and the stories they've written for this issue. Contributing writers aren't on staff, but they write frequently enough to warrant a masthead mention. Often, magazines have a contributors' page, which carries short biographies of the freelancers in the magazine that month, and also at the end of the article. Read these bios—they'll give you clues as to what types of freelancers the publication hires. What experience do they have, and how does it compare with your own?

Now go through the magazine again; count the number of *departments*, short sections in either the front or back, and notice what they cover. Some departments may be news-oriented; some may have quirky stories; others may contain follow-ups on previously published stories. How many were written by freelancers? What's the tone and topic matter? *Inc. Technology* magazine had a section called Bulletin Board, which included short, quirky pieces (about four hundred words each) having to do with new or unique technologies. Although the focus of the magazine was the application of technology to make a small business more efficient, those short pieces went a bit beyond that stated purpose. In one issue, the magazine wrote about unique laptop cases, software for managing "doggy hotels," and the story of a volunteer for the Sierra Club who built the environmental group's website while at his day job, much to the dismay of his bosses.

Many magazines have an *end page* as well, which they often give to freelancers for a personal experience essay or some other type of soft, entertaining material. Some readers do like to page through a magazine backward.

Next, count the length and number of features in the *feature well.* The well contains the meat of the magazine. It's either in the middle or toward the back, and you'll find all the longer features here. How many features are there? How long are they? A standard magazine page carries between 800 and 1,200 words, depending on the typeface and design. What topics do they cover?

You can tell who a magazine's readers are by looking at the ads. Who does the advertising target? Look at the people depicted in the ad photos for clues to the magazine's target market(s). Are there ads for furs and expensive watches? Or is it car parts and lawnmowers? Are the cosmetics advertised high-end or inexpensive? Are there pharmaceutical ads for arthritis medicine? If you're looking at a technical or trade publication, note whether the advertisers assume a certain level of knowledge in their ads—they don't have to

How to Analyze a Magazine

Before you sell a product to a customer, you spend a lot of time figuring out what that customer needs. Selling your writing to a magazine is exactly the same. You need to know what types of articles the magazine already buys, and how many. The point of this exercise is twofold: to learn about the market so you can pitch stories that will be bought; and to tailor your writing as if it were a product.

Market:

On a piece of paper, answer the following questions about the publication.

1. The audience for this magazine is ___________. Look at the advertising, read the magazine's mission statement (found at the bottom of the masthead or in *Writer's Market*), look at the overall content of the magazine. Do the editors assume the reader has some knowledge of the subject? How many service articles are there, and what do they address?

2. Is there a lot of art? What kind? Who contributed it? Look at the *cutline*—the print below the photo, also known as the caption. Does it appear to be the author's responsibility to provide art (this is the case for many trade publications)?

3. Look at the design: Is the magazine printed on glossy, hard paper stock? Or softer newsprint-type paper? Are there many ads? How are they situated? Is there a lot of sophistication to the design, or is it simple?

4. How many freelancers contributed stories? How many staff writers? How many "contributing" writers or editors?

Content:

Complete this exercise for all of the major features and departments.

1. This story is about __________. Be specific. Don't just write, "This story is about organic food." Write, "This story is about how organic food is becoming popular with unexpected populations." That's called the *angle*, and you should be able to state it succinctly. An editor once said, "If you can't write your idea on the back of my business card, you don't have a good idea."

2. The writer assumes the reader knows ______________. What? Something about the industry, some background? Again, state it clearly.

3. The article's tone is _____________. Breezy? Ominous? Technical? Humorous? Every magazine has a tone, and within that are variations in each article. Note the overall tone, where the editors have varied it, and why.

4. How does the writer achieve this tone? By using what kinds of words and sentence structure? Does the nut graph fall early or late in the story? What word choices did this writer make? Short, pithy sentences or long, technical ones? Does the story end with a quote, trail off, or tie up in a summary paragraph? Does the ending introduce a new idea that might suggest a follow-up story?

explain what a router is, only that you need theirs.

Now that you've looked through the magazine a few times superficially, it's time for the really deep digging. Consider this next step similar to taking a writing class from the magazine's editor.

With a pen and your story map, pick out a few articles similar to those you might write. During this first reading, pay attention to the overall tone, how the subject matter is presented, and how each article ends. Your focus in this part of the exercise will be on content, style, and structure.

Go through the magazine's departments. Count how many words are in the *lead* of each department story. The job of the lead paragraph or paragraphs is to pull the reader into the story and make him or her want to keep reading.

When does the *nut graph* appear? A nut graph is a paragraph that tells you exactly what the article is about. In magazine writing, the nut graph tells the reader what to expect from the story. Some magazines prefer that the nut graph follow directly after the lead, while others allow more background to sneak in between, stretching the lead section into two or three paragraphs.

Do the lead and the nut graph contain the real experiences of people? Are they anecdotal, in other words, setting a scene? Or are they purely informational, providing us with interesting facts right off the bat? What does the writer tell us in the tone of the first few graphs (paragraphs)? Is it breezy, informal, or serious? How do the leads change from article to article? Does every article have a similar tone?

Next, read through the rest of the story. How is the information presented? How much background do we get, or does the writer assume a certain amount of knowledge on the reader's part? Are there a lot of unexplained technical terms? Is the writing dense or light? Are you engaged in the story or skipping ahead? Are the sentences short? Long? Combination?

Once you've drawn your story map, try applying it to other articles in the magazine. You'll likely find that each article of similar size shares characteristics.

Now that you've noted what the editors are looking for in each type of article, you're ready to seriously pitch a story idea.

Types of Publications

Trade Publications

Many businesspeople-turned-writers find great success writing for *trade publications* that cover their current or former professions. These publications are, in industry jargon, business-to-business (B2B) publications. That means, from a content standpoint, they assume a certain knowledge on the part of the reader. *Writer's Market*, which lists the titles and writers' guidelines for publications seeking freelance work, counts more than 450 trade publications. Titles cover an amazing array of topics, ranging from *Natural Foods Merchan-*

diser to *Aviation Week* to *Hospital News*. The editors of trade publications often come from the industry on which they report, and those editors, in turn, tend to hire writers with industry knowledge.

Trade publication articles are based on specialized industry knowledge—some like to call it business intelligence. Because they are plugged into the industry, the trades get the news first, and they have extremely close relationships with their sources. Often, trade publications serve as the source for articles you might see in a national publication, and their editors are often called on to serve as experts in those articles.

In our opinion, trade publications are the best place for someone like you to begin your career. Here's why: First, you know your business and its players. You know the best sources and can offer the editors of these publications the opportunity to expand their own lists of contacts. Second, you can write beyond the obvious.

Here's what we mean. Suppose you run a food distribution business. You decide to write an article on how slotting fees affect the bottom line, and what to do about it. In publishing jargon, this is called a *service* piece, an article that gives the reader some new information he or she can use. Because you're in the business, and because you've experienced what slotting fees do to the bottom line and know how *you* solved it, your audience is immediately interested. You speak from experience, which lends authority to your writing. You will, of course, interview other experts for your article and check your facts (see chapter 3, "Research and the Room to Write," and chapter 4, "Turn Your Contacts into Great Interviews").

Your detailed, insider's story is much more valuable to a trade-publication editor than, say, that of a writer who cold-calls to pitch a general story on how natural and organic foods have been increasing in popularity for the past fifteen years. "It's generally pretty obvious when I get a query or a pitch from a writer whether that person has some familiarity, first, with the magazine and, second, with the industry," says Karen Raterman, content editor for the publication *Natural Foods Merchandiser*. "And it is really quite amazing how often we get stories submitted where it is obvious that the person hasn't even seen, let alone read, the magazine."

Trade publications are looking for specifics, tight angles, and an insider's knowledge of the business. They're looking for you.

Just as national magazines have writer's guidelines, so do trade publications. Again, we suggest that you attend trade shows in your targeted industry. Often, a major trade publication hosts the show, and certainly some editors and writers will be there. It is also a great opportunity to find out if your ideas are what they're looking for.

There are plenty of other types of publications out there that need your expertise as an industry professional and as a writer. Some take a little digging to find, others are right under your nose. And they all use freelancers.

Customer Newsletters

Customer Newsletters are one such example. Next time you receive your gas or phone bill, examine the contents of the envelope. You'll likely find, in addition to your bill, a newsletter that contains tips to save electricity, a feature article on some charity the company is contributing to, maybe even an article about the industry. Customer newsletters generally highlight new products, introduce new services, build brand identity, and, the company hopes, inspire customer loyalty. Much of the time, that newsletter is written by a freelancer.

Similarly, the editors of customer newsletters are often looking for freelancers with insider knowledge, and sometimes these people are scarce. Sherry McKinley, who runs The Newsletter Company, a Dallas-based publisher established in 1981, says they do look for people with specialized knowledge, but often can't find them. "We had Lowe's Home Improvement [a newsletter client]," McKinley says. "We posted ads on different URLs, looking for writers with do-it-yourself experience. We got no responses."

Writing marketing, in-house, and customer newsletters can be a lucrative gig for the freelancer with specific expertise. Newsletters, like trade publications, are always looking for good material. Because they are published regularly, newsletters can become the bread-and-butter of a full-time or part-time writing business.

"We have a stable of writers we call regularly, [and we] try to divide out the work, so we don't overload anyone," says McKinley. "Once we get someone trained on a project, we'll keep them forever. We've invested so much in teaching them about the client, the dos and don'ts, the acronyms, you have to screw up pretty badly to lose that job."

The problem is that this work is a little harder to find. Most newsletters, for example, don't post a listing in *Writer's Market*, nor do they have a website. This is where your networking skills come in handy. Generally, the company's marketing department is responsible for the newsletter, although they will often outsource it to their advertising agency, which will, in turn, find another subcontractor to do it. That's how McKinley launched her company—she worked at an ad agency that passed on all the newsletters to her. She enjoyed the work and recognized the market.

Keep in mind that membership associations and other nonprofits produce newsletters for members and benefactors. These organizations are good sources for newsletter writing work as well. Stephanie was the small-business columnist for the Connecticut Business and Industry Association's member newspaper for three years. Writing a two-thousand-word service article each month kept her in touch with the movers and shakers in the state, which helped her find expert story sources for other articles, as well.

Weekly Business Insert

Business journalism has become much more popular among newspaper readers in the past decade or so. And now, nearly every major city's daily newspaper has a *weekly business insert*. Usually they come out on Monday or Tuesday. Generally, they have a feature-style story on the first page, maybe a business profile or two, brief news announcements, and some *wire copy*—an article pulled from a national wire service, such as the Associated Press, that isn't locally oriented. Some have weekly expert columnists. *The Boulder Daily Camera*, for example, publishes a business evaluation expert in its Tuesday, "Business Plus" section.

Weekly inserts and monthly supplements in newspapers generally are a good market for freelancers. Although the editors of these pages may not care so much about your business experience, your insider's knowledge of the industry can help you deliver good ideas. Editors of these publications are usually looking for unique business profiles, but may save the news features for their staff writers. Analyze the publication to figure out which types of articles they farm out to freelancers.

Business Weekly

In addition to the weekly insert, there's a separate *business weekly* (sometimes called a *business journal*) owned and published by an independent company in almost every city. Weeklies are a great market for writers with specialized expertise like yours. Business weeklies (which are B2B publications, like the trades) are hungry for material. Each week they have to fill their newspapers with business news.

Nearly all of these publications have a section called "Focus" (sometimes called "Special Report"), where they address a specific topic, generally weekly. Industry topics might range from tourism to government procurement to manufacturing. The weekly's challenge, then, is to fill the focus pages with well-written, insightful features. Sometimes these sections can be quite large, and editors will be scrambling to fill them. Business weeklies also run small-business and people profiles, stories without a hard-news edge, whose writers don't need to know much about a specific industry. Many times they freelance out these "soft" items so their staff reporters have time to work on their beats.

Each business weekly is slightly different, but they all run under the same general model. It helps to make contact with the managing editor, ask what he or she needs, and find out when the deadlines are. Ask for his or her annual editorial calendar, too, to see which topics are coming up in the months ahead.

National Magazines

Many *national magazines* have business-type articles within their pages. *Working Mother*, for example, publishes one service article per month about working outside the home ("How to Get Along with a Difficult Boss," "How to Run a Professional Meeting"). *Natural Home* magazine has a department called "Nuts & Bolts" that covers energy-efficient and environmentally sound solutions for houses, and how to install them or find a professional who can. *Victoria* magazine, *Woman's Day*, and other women's service publications report on women-owned businesses of interest.

However, publishing business stories is not the main business of these service publications. Aiming for a national magazine right off the bat—even when it is a business magazine like *Fortune*, *Forbes*, or *Fast Company*—is a challenging proposition.

During the first week of Emily's magazine-writing class, she asks her students to bring in a magazine for which they would like to write. By the second class, the room is filled with *Vogue*, *Bon Appétit*, *GQ*, and *Architectural Digest*. Emily is then forced to burst the bubble of those shining stars of enthusiasm. The fact is, national magazines, whether business or consumer, are an incredibly tough beat to get. Many have a stable of regular freelancers, most of whom have been writing for them for years. Some have large staffs, and rarely accept any freelance work at all. They have very specific ideas of what they want in an article and what articles they are looking for.

In our experience, editors at trade publications are more open to suggestions. And although our mission here is to encourage, not discourage, we do want to steer you away, at least in the beginning, from wasting too much time and energy trying to get an article placed in a national magazine. Hone your skills, build your clips, network like crazy. Then pitch to the big dogs.

Types of Articles

Expert Column

This is generally written in the first person and imparts advice to the reader. It is one of the most seriously misunderstood vehicles in all of journalism. In order to write the expert column, you must first be an expert. You must have something to say, and you must be able to say it with lots of originality and panache. Although writing an expert column is an excellent way to develop a file folder of clips, it's not the same as writing a service or news article where you've researched an issue, interviewed a variety of people, and built an article around it. Expert columns contain only the opinion and advice of the writer, for example.

Therefore, to write an expert column, it helps to have a recognizable name in the business. For example, if you've been a mergers-and-acquisitions lawyer in your town for a decade or two, chances are businesspeople know and respect your opinion. It is perfectly acceptable to pitch an expert column to the local business weekly based on your expertise.

However, there are a couple of things to note. Expert columnists rarely get paid. Generally, they write to get their name and expertise in front of as many people as possible. Expert columnists almost always wear another hat—business consultant, attorney, or tax specialist.

Editors receive dozens of free expert columns, and query letters offering them, every week. Generally, each newspaper or magazine has a section devoted to columns. Some rotate, some use the same people every week.

If you want a good example of an expert column, look to Jeffrey Gitomer. He writes a weekly sales-advice column syndicated in hundreds of business publications. Gitomer seeks no additional sources for his columns, and the readers assume a certain expertise on his part because he has written several books in his subject areas. He uses a lot of personal anecdotes to make his columns come alive. Gitomer gets about ten dollars a column from each publication, which, admittedly, adds up to a chunk of change. However, his main goal in writing his columns is to sell his books, tapes, speaking, and consulting services.

The Service Article

Here's where you really get to use your expertise. Typically, editors think of a service article as a kind of how-to piece: the reader walks away with advice, tips, and something interesting or new to apply to his or her own business or life. Most national magazines are rife with service articles. Check out most small-business magazines, like *Inc.* magazine. The editors use case studies to illustrate how an entrepreneur solved a problem. "Here's how Joe overcame lousy sales numbers." Recent *Inc.* cover stories include designing a killer website and advice on how to make your website profitable. The editors have appealed to the reader's insecurities or lack of knowledge and are offering up advice.

The News/Trends Feature

Our personal favorite, the *news/trends feature*—type of article basically "hooks" off a current event and discusses its effect on the industry. For example, years ago, Whole Foods Market did an initial public offering (IPO). It was one of the first companies in the natural foods sector to look to the stock market to fuel its growth. This single event led several other natural foods wholesalers and retailers to look at IPOs. A stock analyst took an interest, and there was an investor's conference.

As news/trends feature on the actual IPO would not have been interesting to an editor—the magazine most certainly would have covered it as straight news. But a news/trends story could have focused on several areas: One possible angle would be how the grass roots, Birkenstock-wearing, tie-dyed, natural foods industry was maturing into suits and ties (metaphorically speaking). Another angle could have been the effect on the suppliers of natural foods when their customers suddenly had to answer to shareholders. Coming up with an interesting trend with a news hook is a feature writer's job.

The Business or Personality Profile

The most important thing to remember about the profile is that its subject must be interesting, special, unique, or odd. Just like the service feature, the profile ideally should have an inherent lesson, or "take away" value to the reader.

Simply writing a profile of Joe Smith and recounting his résumé, starting with elementary school, will bore your reader to death. Instead, focus on how Joe Smith, with his unique personality (which you would illustrate by including tangible details about how Joe behaves around his customers), manages to make every customer a friend—literally. The reader gets an entertaining story about Joe Smith, and the added lesson, "make friends with your customers to build brand loyalty."

Consider a story about how a homebuilder volunteers his time to teach building skills to disadvantaged youths. Then, during a tight labor market, he hires them. It's a good business solution and a great feel-good story. You know who the interesting people are in your business community; you are well on

Types of Articles Editors Most Want to Buy and What You Can Do about It

1. Trend stories: Because editors don't work directly in industry, they're often unaware of up-and-coming trends. Identify a trend in your industry that might not yet be common knowledge.
2. Service articles: You know the best way to solve certain problems in your business. Write a list of problems and solutions you encounter every day. Note which ones have enough substance and importance to turn into a six-step, how-to article.
3. The unique business profile: You probably encounter interesting people in your business on a daily basis. To be a good subject for a profile, that person must have a unique personality, an original way of doing something, or have overcome some kind of difficulty. Make a list of the interesting people you know, and why they'd be good candidates for business profiles.
4. Shorts: These are a great way to break into a magazine. They require less research than the larger pieces and are often the area of a publication that uses the most freelance work. Shorts are tidbits and quirky items that don't quite warrant a full article.

your way to selling an interesting business profile to an editor.

Shorts

Magazines all carry *shorts*—sometimes called departments—either in the front or the back of the publication. Shorts contain quirky, entertaining, or useful information that may not warrant a longer article. Shorts are an excellent way to break into the higher profile consumer magazines because editors are always hungry for them.

Although they are shorter, shorts are not necessarily easier to write. You only have 300 to 500 words to get your point across. But they are a good way to prove your writing ability, your reliability, and your insider's knowledge.

To Do Today

- ☐ Buy a copy of *Writer's Market* or subscribe to the online service.
- ☐ Visit a newsstand and purchase magazines and newspapers that interest you.
- ☐ Call the trade association in your industry and ask which trade publications are popular; get copies of those publications.
- ☐ Study those magazines using the story-map method in this chapter, writing down the angle of each article in the feature, as well.
- ☐ Make a list of potential story topics about which you could write, what the angle might be, who the market is, and why you are the writer to do the piece.

Interview with Karen Raterman,

vice president of content, *Natural Foods Merchandiser,* New Hope Communications.

How much importance do you place on industry knowledge as a criterion for hiring freelancers? Would you look more carefully at a pitch from someone who'd once worked in the natural foods business?

I think industry knowledge is very important, but I wouldn't make that the sole criterion, or even top criterion, for hiring a freelancer. What really impresses me is the freelancer who doesn't necessarily have industry experience but will make a pitch that shows they've done their homework. He or she has read the magazine, understands the industry's issues, know the kinds of angles that we like to use, and has come up with a well thought out and different idea.

We often are approached by people with very strong industry experience or expertise. While this can be a good thing, especially if you are looking for an opinion piece, it can also be problematic. Just because someone has experience as a retailer, an herbalist, or a traveler, that doesn't make them a writer. Probably the most important quality I like to see in a freelancer is solid business writing and reporting experience. If a person has a good understanding of how business works and some experience in reporting and writing business articles, there is a good chance they can deliver what we need.

What types of articles do you like to receive from freelancers? Why?

A personality profile, service piece, or news feature are all good. We always need articulate opinion pieces, but we would rarely pay anything for that.

How do you (or your colleagues) go about adding new freelancers to your stable? How do you find them?

We find them in all kinds of ways, but no one way in particular. Occasionally they send a query or we make contact at trade shows. Some people will send in some good clips. Many contact us and send clips electronically.

The advice I would give here is to write a short, but very good, letter that points out any industry knowledge; experience writing for other, particularly similar, publications; and a couple of thoughts on what the freelancer thinks he or she has to offer this publication. It might be good to emphasize that you have a personal interest in this area and would enjoy working closely with the editor to deliver the kinds of articles he or she is looking for. Then include a few nicely copied and stellar clips, if you have them.◆

3. Research and the Room to Write

Americans are fond of poking fun at our own hyper-busyness. We have all seen the young parents in the TV commercial, focused on collecting everything necessary for that trip to Grandma's house—then realizing, two blocks from home, that they forgot the baby. Or the sitcom businessman who leaves his briefcase behind in a crowded airport, frantically retracing his steps at the expense of his tight schedule, all to the sound of a raucous laugh track. We rush headlong through our lives, then joke about it because, after all, what else can we do?

Businesspeople who want to publish what they write must find a way to slow down and allow themselves room to create the story they have in mind. We are so used to putting out fires, slicing minutes off our commutes, maximizing our investments, and leveraging our opportunities that finding the time and space to write seems a dream. But we submit that if you never find the time to write and publish that article, you'll simply drag the idea of that particular failure around with you through all your busy days. Who needs the extra baggage?

Erica Jong, the best-selling author of *Fear of Flying*, once wrote, "How can I know what I think unless I see what I write?" Writing is a thought process that takes plenty of time and contemplation. You need quiet time to think, enough time to interview people, and the time to do the research that will make your case. Writing—and the preparation that goes into writing—takes time. Accept that fact, and let's get to work.

We promised that we would present the information in this book in the order that you'd need it. Chapter 4 is all about interviewing, and sometimes you will need to talk to people first to find out what to write about. Sometimes you will need to do research first in order to write provocative questions for your interviewees, so consider chapters 3 and 4 to be interchangeable.

In this chapter, we will show you how to crystallize your article idea into a clear slant; how to minimize the time you will need to spend on research; and how to find the time and space to write your story.

Draw It

You may know so much about your field of business that sometimes it is hard to know where to start writing about it. Making a preliminary outline of your article before you begin to write doesn't have to be complicated, and can help you narrow your focus so that your story will be effective. Think of the outline as a skeleton that you will flesh out with research, interviews, and writing.

Just begin by making a box at the top of a blank page. Inside it, write a one-word, general business topic, like "marketing," "employees," "products," or "competition." From that top box, draw a spoke and another box. Within that secondary box, write a smaller topic connected to the larger topic. If you're in a retail sales business, for example, an outgrowth of "marketing" might be "e-commerce."

You've already taken a topic that affects all businesses—"marketing"—and narrowed it down to a focus—"e-commerce"—that you can write about within the context of the retail industry.

Now, write down questions about e-commerce in the retail industry as they occur to you. How has e-commerce affected the way your company does business? How do you envision it affecting sales and revenues in the future? Do your brick-and-mortar customers also shop online? How do your colleagues and competitors use e-commerce? What do the experts say about the benefits of e-commerce? Do they agree or disagree?

Sit back and look at what you've drawn. It's an outline for an entire article. If you want to narrow the topic further, go back to the second box and draw a third one from it on an even smaller focus before you begin listing questions. If your word-count assignment is small—fewer than 1,500 words, for example—each question could be an in-depth article on its own.

Try this exercise over and over with other topics, until you feel you have developed a knack for it. Editors look for writers who can condense a story idea into a specific slant or focus. "Retail marketing" is too big a subject to tackle within the bounds of a 1,500-word feature article. "The uses of e-commerce in retail sales" is much more manageable.

Read It

If you are writing about your field of business, once again you have an advantage, this time in the area of research. You already know many sources of information on your subject, including websites, books, experts, and centers of influence. Researching the background information you will need to form interview questions and write your story might seem like a fairly easy task.

It is also an awe-inspiring responsibility. Readers will rely on you for accurate, objective information. As the story continues its life in publication, other writers may use your article as source material. Colleagues and competitors will read it. Even if you think you know your subject cold, check your facts. Fact checking is your duty, not the editor's. A busy copy editor may not catch your errors or misstatements, but it is almost certain that an alert reader will. Your reputation as a writer, and your readers' trust in you, is at stake every time your byline goes beneath a headline. Take your responsibility for accurate reporting seriously.

That said, let's go to the World Wide Web, the first place you'll look for information and statistics to flesh out your story. Use your favorite search engine, whether it's www.yahoo.com, www.hotbot.com, or www.google.com, and use them all to find tidbits of information you might have missed in your first pass.

As an experienced businessperson, you already know who the experts are in your industry, you know which sources are considered reputable. After all, you might do your own research in some form or another almost every day. We're simply going to describe some types of websites that might be useful in your research.

There are certain types of websites that will be especially useful. Industry websites can include membership associations and unions, government agencies that regulate or oversee your industry, and trade publications. These are a good source of statistics and opinions on the most up-to-date issues. Media websites like CNN, the *Washington Post*, MSNBC, and *Time* give you the news. It's a good idea to check the news for the latest slants on the subject you're writing about. Current news stories can give you a good hook to hang your story. Company websites contain the latest news in the form of press releases and often have a media kit for writers to download. Look for links on these pages labeled "Press Room," "Media," "Press Releases," or "Marketing and Communications." These sections are often found under the "About Our Company" heading. General research sites are a treasure trove of information on all kinds of subjects, and they are fun to use. They include the Library of Congress, Encarta (an atlas, dictionary, and encyclopedia in one), Statistical Abstract of the United States, and Bartlett's Familiar Quotations. Government websites are, of course, often useful in business writing. The Securities and Exchange Commission, the Department of Labor, OSHA, and the Environmental Protection Agency (EPA) are often-used sites. State and city government websites also will be helpful if you are writing for a local or regional publication. All of these sites will have links to other webpages relevant to their subject matter. You could spend days delving.

A word of caution: Like a chainsaw, the Internet is both a wonderful and a terrifying tool. While it contains vast amounts of fascinating information, it is also a bit of a free-for-all. Anyone can post anything at any time. That means that much of the information on the Internet comes from questionable sources and has questionable validity. If you're using information from an official site, like OSHA or EPA, you can be certain it's good data. You also can go to many reliable Internet sources for information on your industry, and you already know which ones to trust. But other, randomly discovered sites may contain erroneous information. Before using research you've found on the Net, verify it with a couple of knowledgeable sources.

The Associated Press Stylebook and Briefing on Media Law (Perseus Publishing, Cambridge, Mass., 2000) contains outstanding sections on how to use the Internet as a reference resource and how to check Internet sources. It is the bible for many of us who edit and write for newspapers, and we have listed its information in the "Suggested Reading List" on page 125.

Park It

If 98 percent of success is just showing up, then showing up is 100 percent of writing. Whether you're interviewing other people or simply writing from your own experience, you have got to put in the time it takes to get full and complete answers to your questions. This may mean doing some research, either on the Internet or in a library. Depending on your focus and its depth, you might have to interview other experts in your field. Even if you've chosen a topic with which you are very familiar, you'll want to check the latest news on the subject to make sure your facts are up-to-date.

And then there's the actual writing time. You might be able to write a press release or your grocery list in the middle of a staff meeting, but an article is another story. Allow yourself time to write, rewrite, and show your writing to an informed reader or two. It doesn't matter if you are writing in the cathedral hush of a research library, or with the kids barricaded and bribed into staying in the next room. It all happens inside your head anyway.

Sit yourself in a chair, and take the time and space to write. After fifteen years as a freelance writer working at home in many different cities and houses, Stephanie believes that décor is negotiable. Comfort is not. Dress down. Gather your tools, supplies, outline, and research. Close the door. Type one word, and the next will follow. Stretch when you're tired, and keep going as long as you can. If the writing part of your brain gets tired, distract yourself by checking a few facts or making a few phone calls. Go back to the writing. Get a feel for your output—this many hours will produce this many words. Pat yourself on the back. And once in a while, get out of the house.

Offline and Out the Door: What a Reference Librarian Can Do for You

If the last time you used a library was for a high-school biology paper, it may be time to revisit your local branch. Libraries are a storehouse of free information for business writers. Whether you want to access the Internet, read up on issues in your field, or find out who buys what you want to publish, the library is still a great place to do your homework.

Public library systems have many resources and features to help you research your articles. Your local research librarian is the best of these resources. He or she can point you toward the information you need.

Delegating your biggest research question to a research librarian gives you a virtual staff on your busiest day. Believe us, at this very moment there is a research librarian who is bored by the same old homework questions and longs to sink her impeccably educated teeth into something interesting. You can drop by in person, call, or ask your questions through the website provided by your local public library (allow at least three days for the answer). You also can connect to the online catalog from your home computer at the same website

Jump In! Three Simple Steps from Beginning to Byline

1. Draw it.

Sketch out your article before you research, interview, and write. Pick a general heading, like "economic development." Make the next heading within that topic smaller in focus, like "economic development in Connecticut." Then list questions under the second, smaller topic. "Which agencies drive economic development in Connecticut? What are their areas of responsibility? Expertise? How do their strategies compare with, or differ from, each other? Are there overlapping missions? Could some of these agencies be consolidated for improved effectiveness? What do the people running these agencies have to say about such a consolidation? What do others have to say about it? Is there a movement afoot to bring about that consolidation?" And so on. You will end up with enough points to write a comprehensive article of 1,500 words or more.

2. Park it.

Clear your schedule, and find a quiet space to research and write. Many writers with other jobs get up early to find an extra hour on weekday mornings, or set aside a few hours on the weekend. Others can switch gears when they get home from work and give up their evening hours to write. Explain your commitment to your family and get them on board, too. If your family life is just too hectic, you might consider writing outside the home. Although Emily and Stephanie each have a room dedicated to writing in their homes, they appreciate a change of scenery. Emily writes in the morning hours, before work, sometimes waking at 6:30 A.M. and writing until 8:30 A.M. She also sets aside a few hours each weekend day. Stephanie sometimes prefers the hush of the Special Collections Branch of the Rio Grande Valley Library System. All you need are the basic tools you use for writing, and some degree of comfort and quiet.

3. Publish it.
When it comes to publishing articles in your area of expertise, you are your own best marketer. Publications that you read regularly for news about your industry are looking for writers who can handle assignments on industry topics. They are looking for good ideas from the right writer. You have to let them know you're available. Refer to chapter 1, "Network, Don't Query," for specific advice on how to contact an editor about publishing your work.

address to find individual books and their locations, thereby saving yourself time when you get there.

If you can't access the Internet at your home or office, you can at the library. Depending on how busy the branch is, you can stay on the computer from fifteen minutes to one hour. Your library might allow you to make an appointment for Internet time.

Library guidelines caution users about the validity of the information they might find on the Internet, and we do, too. Ask your reference librarian questions regarding the accuracy of sources. At some branches, volunteers and/or librarians provide basic Internet instructions. Printouts cost pennies per page, and you can bring your own floppy disc on which to download materials.

The vast amount of printed matter at your local library also provides many low-tech sources for business-article research. If you want to fortify that mailing or contact list with sources of expert interviewees, check the business reference table for *The Thomas Registers*, or *Hoover's Handbook of American Business, Emerging Companies, and World Business*. The *D & B Million Dollar Directory*, from Dun & Bradstreet, can provide you with detailed information on the sales and operations of America's prominent public and private companies, as well as the names of top management. All of these references are available online as well. Some charge a hefty fee for all but the most basic information, and others are entirely free. Most library branches have a copy of *Who's Who in America*. You can find sources for local contacts in the library too, including phone books from all over the state.

Periodicals can keep you up-to-date on the latest issues and current events in your field, and provide you with valuable how-to information. The main branch of a public library system might hold an extensive periodicals archive, and most branches contain current newspapers from major U.S. cities. The automated card catalog on the library's computer can help you find the publications and articles you are looking for.

If your branch librarian can't help you find the information you need, he or she may refer you to another local institution, such as a business library or other special collection. Whatever your inquiry or informational need, you can be sure that your library can point you in the right direction. They answer thousands of research questions each year.

There is yet another reason why any busy businessperson/writer might want to visit the library—for its stress management capabilities. It's quiet, comfortable, and somebody else cleans up after you. Leave the cell phone back at the office.

To Do Today

- ☐ Practice honing article slants using the exercise under the "Draw It" section of the sidebar on page 34. Keep a notebook of your exercises. You can come up with story outlines that will give you plenty of ideas to pitch to an editor.
- ☐ Bookmark the best websites in your industry. Add websites for general business information to the list of sites you frequently visit.
- ☐ Introduce yourself to your local research librarian. Ask about the services he or she can provide. Give him or her one good question to research for your next article.
- ☐ Find a quiet place and time to write. Use chapter 5, "Building a Strong Structure," to shape your story.

The Wonderful Web

By no means a comprehensive list, here are some of our favorite general sites for researching and writing business articles:

www.bizjournals.com
Local business news from forty-two cities. A wonderful place to look up trend stories (go to the "Industries" link).

www.bloomberg.com
If you are writing about publicly traded companies, Bloomberg is a great resource for tracking stocks, finding industry analysts' recommendations, and looking up news. You can get Securities and Exchange Commission documents on www.sec.gov, but Bloomberg gives you the news and analysis. Also good for industry-trend articles.

www.businessweek.com
The magazine plus special sections, online.

www.djinteractive.com (Dow Jones Interactive)
A powerful media research engine, it requires a subscription and is worth every penny.

www.freelunch.com
Need a national demographic factoid? Want to insert the history of the prime rate over the past six months? Freelunch.com has oodles of national data for sprinkling into stories.

www.hoovers.com
Basic information on private companies is available free. This is a good place to start when you're looking for phone numbers, addresses, CEOs' names, and a basic idea of what a company does. It's expensive to go deeper into the site, but may be worth it for some writers.

www.ire.org (Investigative Reporters and Editors, Inc.)
If you write regularly for a publication, it pays to become a member. They train journalists, and offer invaluable help for story ideas, research, and writing in many areas.

www.osha.gov (Occupational Safety & Health Administration)
Their *Job Safety & Health Quarterly* magazine can be downloaded in pdf format. It is chock-full of information about workplace safety in high-hazard industries, and timely topics like workplace violence and anthrax.

www.prnewswire.com and www.businesswire.com
Both of these sites run press releases and are good places to see basic company news.

www.sej.org (Society of Environmental Journalists)
You can gather lots of information here without being a member. If you write about environmental concerns in your industry or state, their TipSheet is an unparalleled source of ideas and information.

Also available online: Local bankruptcy and public court documents. Search the website of your local or federal court clerk by date to find out who's gone bust recently. Cross-reference the names with your local or federal judicial district to find out who was sued.

Interview with Josh Hyatt,

executive editor, *Fortune Small Business* magazine, published by Time, Inc.

If I know so much about my topic, why must I research the subject and talk to other experts for my article? Isn't my expertise enough?

You can't be objective—or, even if you can, you can't appear to be objective.

Presumably, if you are in a certain business, you feel you know better than your competitors. At the very least, you have a certain point of view on how things should (and shouldn't) be done. Think of the stock market: there are tons of so-called "experts," and they all say something different.

Here's a side benefit: you'll get a wider perspective on what you think you know so well. There's always more to be learned.

How do professional writers check their sources and their facts?

The best way to check facts is to have at least two sources for every fact. In other words, as smart as you may be, your word is not enough. Particularly CEOs, who are used to being in sales mode, will often be surprised when they find out the truth about the "facts" they regularly deploy. This is partly why they are usually unhappy about what journalists write.

How do I know that I've covered all the bases in researching my subject? Is there such a thing as over-researching?

When people start repeating stuff you've already heard, that's generally the time to stop. Until then, you keep bouncing the facts you learn from one person off the next. Sooner or later, you find yourself traveling, factually, in a circle.

Will you share a research tip?

My number one tip (for free!): the last question of any interview should always be, "Is there anything I should have asked you—but didn't?" You'll be surprised at what you don't know enough to ask.◆

4. Turn Your Contacts into Great Interviews

You are the expert. That's the message we've been sending in chapters 1, 2, and 3—that your business experience is the jumping-off point to a writing career.

But here we are at chapter 4 and we've got more news for you: You are not *the* expert.

Any article you publish in a trade journal, popular magazine, or newspaper will begin with an idea. That idea is born from your knowledge of the industry you're covering, or your experience of the business world in general.

However, unless you are offered an opinion column or an assignment to write an editorial, you must get your information for the article from other sources.

Between us, we interview hundreds of businesspeople every year. We had tons of information to put into this chapter, as you can imagine, and little idea of how to organize it. So we decided to go back to the five *W*s (who, what, when, where, and why) and the *H* (how). This way, we gave our chapter a structure, and at the same time, we can give you a crash course in basic journalism.

Here's the big *why* of interviewing story sources: Journalists have to follow the story. We don't decide what that story is first, and then go out and get it. We get the story by talking to others—first.

One person never knows the whole story. A few people on different sides of the issue can give a clearer picture. Cover your beat, talk to those people again and again, and the whole story will begin to emerge.

The Big Who

You already know whom to call for news and expert information about your industry. You know the major companies, professional organizations, and individual players who make the business world, or your part of it, revolve. When you're writing an article about your industry, you must interview those major players.

Let's say you are going to write an article about a merger in the energy industry. Talking to one side—the buyer—is not enough. For balanced coverage—the why of the deal—you must speak with the other side and, naturally, you would. Your original sources are the press releases and other materials listed on both companies' websites under "Media," "Press Package," or "Reporters." The press releases will have the name of a media, marketing, or public-relations contact. Start there.

But suppose that merger has implications for the entire industry. For example, because Company A and Company B are joining forces, the consolidation of their products and/or services presents other players with a larger, more serious competitor.

Your circle of interviewees widens to include a business expert who can speak about the implications this merger has for the energy industry as a whole. If the

Summary

Writing an article about a business subject without talking to the major players is like watching actors sit, speechless, on a stage while somebody else reads the play. In addition to letting the major players talk, you might expand the article's scope by calling on:

1. Business experts in the subject or industry
2. Minor players (like competitors, suppliers, neighbors, onlookers)
3. Government experts in the subject
4. Professional organizations in the industry
5. Academic experts in the subject
6. Other writers on the subject
7. Centers of influence

company is publicly traded, analysts that cover the company's stock, or the industry, are excellent expert sources. They, after all, write research reports about the industry.

If your assigned word count for the story is, for example, 2,500 words instead of 1,000 words, you might have room to include interviews with minor players, like competitors and vendors, about their perceptions of what this merger does to the playing field.

If there are regulatory or other matters involved in the merger, you should talk to government experts in the appropriate local, state, regional, or federal department.

Suppose the membership of a professional association in the energy industry has an opinion on the subject of this particular merger. Talk to them, too.

If there is a new medical, scientific, or educational aspect, perhaps one company wanted to acquire the other because of this new development. (A good example would be a new discovery or development in the energy field.) Many of the people you could interview about the technical aspects of this discovery or development can be found among academic experts. Don't worry that you won't understand the technical aspects: academics are teachers and, contrary to the "ivory tower" cliché, they almost always make great interviews.

Occasionally you will speak with other writers on the subject. A person who has written books on mergers and acquisitions would be a good resource for this example article. If you are especially identified with the particular subject— if you're writing about the need to keep your sources confidential, and the name of your article is "Deep Throat Was Elvis," and you just happen to know Bob Woodward—by all means, interview him if your word count assignment allows it.

Centers of influence are people who can multiply your contacts in a five-minute conversation. You already know them, or can meet them at networking and social events. They include retired executives, public-relations professionals, business consultants, and anyone who fits into the general category of someone-who-knows-everyone. They are the people you can always call on to explain what you're looking for, and they can plug you into all of the people you must interview to get the whole story. You can even speak with that person off the record to get background information that might not be otherwise available in your research.

What, When, and Where: Face-to-Face or over the Phone?

Some business people are shy of reporters and interviews. They watch *Hard Copy* and Barbara Walters, and they think you're going to sensationalize what they say, or try to make them cry.

At the other extreme, some people think the article is going to be about them, when it's really about a topic or an event. For an article on trends in estate planning, Stephanie called an expert, an attorney in Connecticut, to set up a twenty-minute telephone interview. His secretary called back—the man wanted to know if Stephanie would be bringing the camera crew with her, or if they would be scheduling a separate time for the photo shoot. The man had gone from "estate planning expert" to "rock star" in the space of a short phone call.

For so many reasons, you should let your sources know the scope of your story, or as much as is possible at the time of the interview. Give your interviewees a storyline—a one- or two-sentence synopsis of the article, and their role in it. Tell them when your deadline is. It's important to let the source know that you plan to cover his or her story fairly and accurately, and hearing his or her side of it is the only way that's going to happen. Make it known at the outset that, unless he or she tells you otherwise, everything that is said or that happens during the interview is on the record.

It's important to put the source at ease. Sometimes it's easier to do that face-to-face than over the phone. One former *New Mexico Business Weekly* reporter, Karen Jarnagin, always interviews in person. She's an attractive and personable individual who's got an amazing way of making people feel at ease. She always begins an interview with a few minutes of small talk—the weather, her family, just some words to make her source understand that she, too, is a real person, not just a reporter. People say the darnedest things to her.

How, Now

Prepare your questions from research and any preliminary talks with the players, major and minor, on or off the record (see our sidebar "Twenty-Five Questions to Ask Any Business" on pages 46–47). Pick up the phone and start calling.

Tap into your own well-developed skills to conduct the interview. You have briefed colleagues, presented proposals to clients, interviewed prospective employees, negotiated with higher-ups, crushed competitors with a few well-chosen words. Your interviewing techniques are far superior to those of most beginning writers.

A word or two of caution: take deep breaths, and modulate your voice. Smile. Be respectful in demeanor. Play back your first interview tape to see how you sound. Make adjustments as necessary. For example, Stephanie wasn't aware that she laughed like a hyena, and in all the wrong places, until she heard herself do it on tape.

Make sure that, at the end of the interview, you ask the person if you may call with follow-up questions as you are writing the story.

Don't cut the interview short when you think you have all the information you need. Sometimes the best information comes at the end, when the interviewee is "off guard." Emily once spent two days with a Cuban couple in Miami, business owners who owned some of the first two-way radio/cell-phone devices and used them extensively. They were charismatic and talkative, but she wasn't getting a sense of how the technology fit into their lives, the whole point of the story.

Then, at dinner in a restaurant on the final night of her stay, it happened. The couple's five-year-old daughter's voice squawked through the phone, "Mommie? When are you coming home?" And just like that, Emily had a great, on-point and poignant close for the story.

Shorthand, Scribbling, and the Photographic Memory

One of Stephanie's former clients was a small-town newspaper with a circulation of about eighteen thousand, for which she wrote feature articles, business news, and a book column. The editor was a former newspaper reporter who had retired from the daily grind, become bored at home, and gone back to work at this part-time job.

The editor was a good writer and a great person to work for, especially since she knew all about the ups and downs of the working journalist.

But being in her company was a bit wearing; the woman was an "echo talker." She repeated everything anyone said to her—as they were saying it. Stephanie would begin, "I was wondering if . . . ," and the woman would repeat, "I was wondering if . . . ." It was a strange conversational tic, and the editor did it constantly, whether the conversation was about professional or personal matters.

One day, the editor mentioned that, during her career as a reporter, she had never learned shorthand, and had to write down everything her interviewees were saying. Stephanie, a staunch devotee of the handheld tape recorder, finally

Twenty-Five Questions to Ask Any Business

Sometimes all you need to get the ball rolling is to ask the first question. Here are a few to get you started:

The Basics

1. Please characterize for me what your business does.
2. How long has the company been in business?
3. Who owns the business?
4. What are your annual revenues?
5. How many employees do you have?
6. Is this your only location?
7. Who are your customers?
8. Who are your competitors?
9. What is your mission statement?

The Strategy

10. What is the most important business decision you've ever made? Why?
11. What were the consequences of that decision?
12. At which moment did you know that this change would happen? How did you feel?
13. What series of events led you to this point?
14. What is the biggest business problem you've ever solved?
15. Which trends are affecting your marketplace today?
16. Which factors will affect your business/industry over the next five years?
17. How has technology changed your business?
18. What do your competitors have to say about your success?
19. If someone were starting a similar business today, what tips would you give for that new business owner?
20. Who was your mentor?
21. Which values and influences started you down this path?
22. Excluding people within your company or industry, where do you get your best advice now?

The Closers

23. Which professional associations do you belong to? (Such organizations are a good source for statistics and other research about the industry.)
24. Is there anything else I should know about this topic that I haven't covered?
25. Whom else should I talk to about this subject/industry? (Get at least two other phone numbers.)

realized that this handy device hadn't been available when the woman was writing for newspapers. The editor bought time to scribble quotes accurately by repeating everything her interviewees said.

Happily, technology makes the task much easier for us. Get yourself two tape recorders, one to bring with you on face-to-face interviews, and one that hooks up to your phone. Ask permission to tape, and get the permission *on* tape. Archive your (labeled) tapes for a reasonable time after the article is published, in case your editor, a reader, or an interviewee has a question or concern about what was said during the interview.

Fair warning, however: technology fails on occasion so make sure you also take accurate notes during the interview. Emily once interviewed the CEO of Stoneyfield Farm Yoghurt Company in his car on his way to work. Because she gets car sick, she taped the interview instead of taking notes. During the interview, the CEO rolled down his car window. When she went to listen to transcribe the tape, it was almost incomprehensible because of the wind. Emily was forced to write the interview from memory, then verify again with the CEO. Embarrassing, to say the least.

On the other hand, as you become more skilled with interviewing, you may develop a kind of concentration that will make it possible for you to capture what is necessary for a story without writing down everything a source says. To put a source at ease during a face-to-face interview, it is sometimes necessary to put down the notebook and give that person your full attention. Be absolutely focused on what the person is saying. As you become more skilled at listening during an interview, you will develop your concentration. Occasionally, jot down a sentence or a keyword that will spur your memory. After the interview, rush back to your notebook and fill in the blanks.

This technique is not recommended for everybody, and it is not a technique that works well for technical or number-laden articles. However, it works very well with the "softer" material, such as in recording a person's mannerisms, for color in a profile.

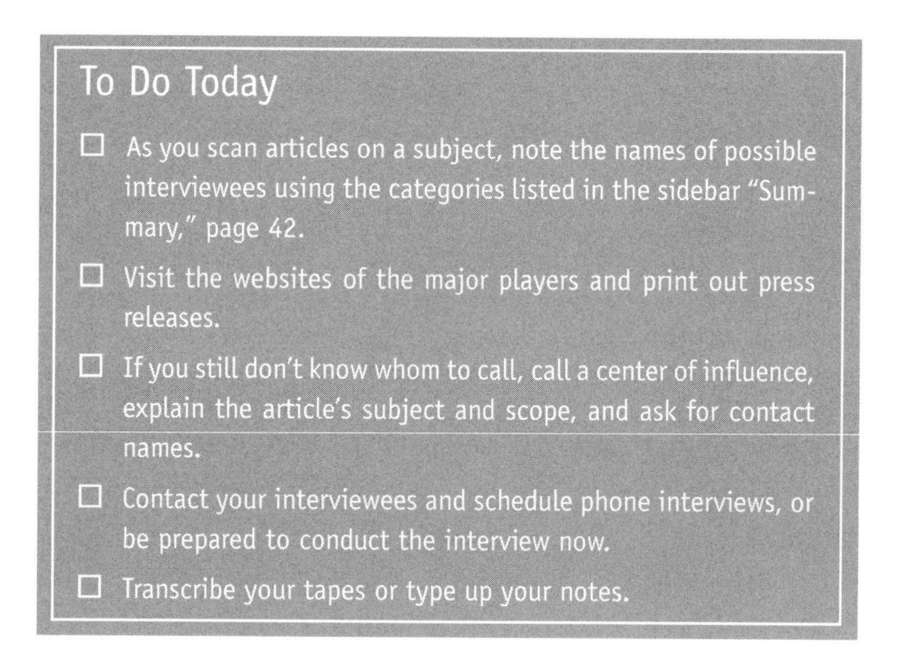

To Do Today

- ☐ As you scan articles on a subject, note the names of possible interviewees using the categories listed in the sidebar "Summary," page 42.
- ☐ Visit the websites of the major players and print out press releases.
- ☐ If you still don't know whom to call, call a center of influence, explain the article's subject and scope, and ask for contact names.
- ☐ Contact your interviewees and schedule phone interviews, or be prepared to conduct the interview now.
- ☐ Transcribe your tapes or type up your notes.

Interview with Will McNamara,

public affairs officer for Sempra, a global energy company, and former editor of *SourceBook Weekly Online*, an international trade journal for energy company executives and other interested readers.

Suppose I am hired by a trade journal to write a business article on an energy topic—let's say, a report on the effects of deregulation on municipal power authorities. Where, in general, do I begin to find interviewees among experts on the subject?

My first step is always to start with my primary research mechanism. I have become a big fan of Dow Jones Interactive, which is a subscription-based research service. There are many similar services. They essentially maintain a database of all the leading newspapers and periodicals in the United States (and, to a lesser extent, foreign countries). A reporter can search through a broad database or specifically target certain publications.

When you are searching a topic in the energy industry, typically you will come upon the same national experts who often speak about a particular subject, so you will find great leads for interviews. The fact that these experts have been quoted in other publications indicates that they are willing to participate in interviews and be directly quoted. In my view, this is one of the best ways to find national experts and determine issues on which they have already been quoted.

A second approach would be to contact one of the national organizations, such as the Edison Electric Institute (EEI) or the American Public Power Association. These organizations certainly have their own points of view, but can be helpful in that they are tracking national issues.

When a reporter is writing about something that is very specific and not nationally focused, a good resource is the press material that a company may release with an announcement. Every large company operating in the energy space should have a media-relations department. The reporter can contact the media representative for information and quotes, which of course should always be balanced with a more objective perspective.

There are literally hundreds of newsletters that cover the energy industry, many of which are available online for free. Reporters who regularly cover the industry should become familiar with energy publications, which will also identify good sources on the given topic.

How do I know I am interviewing the "right" person for the article? Are there a number of "right" people I can interview on a given subject?

I would define "right person" for an interview as anyone who is knowledgeable on the given subject matter. It will then be the reporter's responsibility to ensure that all points of view on the subject are represented in the final article.

It is *never* a good idea to rely on only one source for an article. Even in company profiles, I always instruct writers who are working for me to make sure that they attempt to conduct interviews with the company's competitors so that the final article is well balanced and objective.

The kiss of death for any reporter writing for the energy industry (or any industry, for that matter) would be to do a piece that comes off as being heavily promotional. A reporter would lose all credibility if he or she took an interview at face value without getting a contrary point of view, or appear to be promoting a particular position or company. The objective of any seasoned reporter is to present a balanced, factual article that presents all sides of a given issue and allows the reader to make up his or her own mind.

For a national or international publication, is it important that my interviewees be selected from many different places? Why or why not?

Unless the subject of your article is very focused on a particular place, I think it is always preferable to have interviewees from different places, as different regions often produce different perspectives. Let's use the example of California, where a major energy crisis was covered extensively in the news for most of 2000. People in California have one perspective on the energy crisis, while people in other areas of the country see it very differently. A reporter working on an article about the California energy crisis would want to make sure he or she obtains interviews from a diverse cross section of people.

Should I always strive for in-person interviews, geography permitting? Are email interviews acceptable? Do most interviews take place over the phone?

Less than 5 percent of the interviews that we conduct for our publication take place in person. In-person interviews may be preferable as it always helps to gauge the interviewee's facial expressions, mannerisms, etc. However, the energy industry has truly become a global marketplace and in-person interviews are usually not feasible given the tight deadlines that normally go with a timely publication.

Reporters today have the benefit of technology. Most interviews can take place via the phone, email, and/or fax. We conduct most of our interviews over the phone and use a tape recorder for accuracy.

We use email for follow-up questions and to obtain supporting documents. I don't think it is advisable to conduct the whole interview over email, as the interviewee's responses may become overly rehearsed and prepared. Interviewing by phone is convenient, and you also retain the spontaneity that is so important in gaining new information.◆

5.

Building a Strong Structure

Part of the power of any essay lies in the momentum you create, one point building on another, continuing on toward the conclusion. Structure helps you maintain that momentum, pull the reader in, and keep him or her reading. It supports the type of article you are writing, the slant and attitude of that article, and the ideas you offer within it.

Writing persuasive articles requires a strong framework on which to nail ideas, information, and memorable quotes. Just like carpentry, writing requires a set of tools, a frame or a plan, and the skills to put it all together. Even the best, most well-researched ideas fall flat if their execution is disorganized or illogical. We have all faced a pile of research and been overwhelmed by it. Here, we'll show you how to build the right framework for the information and slip all the pieces into place.

Two of the best gauges of structure are 1) the type of article you are writing and 2) word count. For assistance in analyzing the different types of stories you may be writing—service article, expert column, news/trends feature, profile, or department piece—review chapter 2, "What the Market Will Bear." When thinking about structure, it also helps to look at models of the kind of article you will be writing. If you are beginning an expert column, read other column writers to get an idea of how closely they stick to their subject, and how they make every word work. Read feature articles in your subject area to get a feel for how the length and the flow can vary with word count and topic. Note how lively and information-packed department items are.

Word count helps you determine structure simply because you only have a certain space in which to fit a story. A 1,000-word article is fairly short, a basic five-paragraph essay. A 3,000-word article will require more investigation into its subject. A 750-word column will have a sharp focus and a linear form.

When you get your first assignment, ask the editor to suggest examples of similar work he or she recently has published.

> **What the Market Will Bear**
>
> Here's a recap of the top types of stories that editors buy, from chapter 2:
>
> 1. Expert column
> 2. Service article
> 3. News/trends feature
> 4. Business or personality profile
> 5. Shorts, or department pieces

In this chapter, we give you tips and tricks for writing leads and endings, what to do with "the muddle in the middle," and housekeeping hints to clean up your writing habits.

Leading Techniques

A good lead will grab your readers and drag them (willingly) into your story. It will give them just enough information to tease them, but not enough to overwhelm them. Here are five techniques that work for us and for many business writers and editors.

Scare 'Em

This is our favorite way to begin a news/trends feature. Here is the "Scare 'Em" technique in a nutshell: "You may not know it, but you already have a problem. Never fear, we're going to tell you how to solve the problem you didn't know you had and tell you where to get help. But you have to keep reading."

Stephanie's article "Bad Driving Records Could Put a Big Dent in Your Business Day" relied on the "Scare 'Em" technique to draw in the reader:

> Last month's terrible traffic accident in which four visitors to this state were killed by another driver brought out three hard facts. The driver responsible for the fatal accident was report-

> edly drunk, had prior DWI convictions and, although off-duty at the time, he was driving a vehicle he normally drove for work.

The article went on to detail the consequences for business owners of allowing employees with bad driving records to operate company cars and trucks. Any reader who owned a business fleet was given fair warning by the lead.

Another article began "Many companies last reviewed their employee handbooks when the Family and Medical Leave Act (FMLA) was passed into law in 1993. . . . But if 1993 was the last time you looked at the manual you hand out to employees, experts say it's past time for another review." Again, if you don't read this article, the lead implies, you will be missing valuable information.

Cite Startling Statistics

A close relative of the "Scare 'Em" technique, this opening can motivate your audience to read an article.

Stephanie's feature article on marketing to Hispanics started off with figures from the 2002 U.S. Census. Readers found out in the first paragraph that Hispanics are the fastest-growing group in America, that they've had a 23 percent growth in income since the last Census, and that there are more than two million Hispanic-owned businesses with total revenues of about $300 billion. A business owner looking to expand or strengthen an existing sales niche would be intrigued by these facts.

Place Them at the Scene

One of the freshest ways to begin a story is with a quote and/or description that puts the reader at the scene of the face-to-face interview you conducted.

Stephanie used the following opening for an article about architectural projects in New Mexico that employ the principles of New Urbanism, a new/old idea that promotes walkable neighborhoods and pedestrian-friendly planning:

> Bill Dennis has no trouble answering questions about new urbanist design. "We have clients who come here and say, 'Will this work?' and we say"—he pauses to make a sweeping gesture that takes in all of Old Town Plaza in Albuquerque—"it's only worked for 300 years."

The architect's quote nailed a central idea in the story—that New Urbanism is an old concept. A handy example of New Urbanism, Old Town Plaza in Albuquerque, is right outside his office window, reinforcing the fact that he practices what he preaches. Use of the present tense, a fiction technique adopted by many news publications, puts the reader in the moment. Describing the gesture and the setting makes the experience seem real to the reader. In fewer than fifty words, the person reading the story has all of the information he or she needs to make the decision to keep on reading.

Start with Anecdotal Evidence

For opening a story with style, a good anecdote can't be beat. (This technique can be a close relative of "Place Them at the Scene.")

> When Bill Aberman was running his job-fair business, BPI, in the late 1970s and the 1980s, he often hobnobbed with government officials—but never with a first lady. Yet in July he had the opportunity to hand a flyer about his successor company, Personnel Strategies Inc., to Hillary Rodham Clinton.

That's how Emily began her story for *Inc.* magazine's Inc 500 issue, "Wisdom Won the Hard Way," about how Aberman's company got out of the federal-government-as-sole-client business and diversified its customer base. Meeting Mrs. Clinton was a good story, but Emily made it better by tying it into Abe-rman's former business, then implying how far he'd come with his new venture.

Ask the Reader a Question

This technique for writing a lead gets the reader thinking about which answers the article might offer.

> The venue is booked, the menu is selected, the date is firm. Packing the place is the next item on your list. A great speaker would fill the hall and guarantee good press coverage. But where do you look for a recognized name, an expert in your industry, or a top performer who can keep your audience enthralled for the length of a keynote speech?

Stephanie's story for meeting and convention planners went on to explain the value of booking a speaker through a bureau or an agency.

Just Tell Us

"Internet companies come, and Internet companies go, sometimes in a blaze of unpaid debt, lawsuits, and angry customers." That's the beginning of a news article that Emily wrote for *New Mexico Business Weekly* about a local Internet service provider (ISP) that had criminal complaints filed against it for embezzlement and fraud.

Notice that she started with the most salient facts—that this ISP was on its way out, leaving a trail of trouble behind. Notice what she did not do—begin with a history of the company, leading up to current events. The "Just Tell Us Method" does not start at the beginning. In fact, starting at the beginning is the fastest way to kill reader interest, and one of the most common mistakes that beginning writers make. Open with the present-day story. Fill in any relevant historical details later.

The "Just Tell Us" lead also can be narrative or descriptive, a more leisurely way to introduce your subject if you have an assignment with a larger word count. Stephanie wrote this opening for a profile of a developer who located his residential acreage along the Turquoise Trail in New Mexico:

> Highway 14 is a panoramic corridor that winds up through the Sandia mountains between Albuquerque and Santa Fe. Beautiful, abundant, but a corridor just the same. Many people who drive it are on their way to one city or another, awed by the scenery but merely passing through. Robert Gately wants to flag them down.

The lead paragraph portrays the remote character of the place and suggests the unusual location for this upscale development.

Middling Around

Here is the simple structure imbedded in most magazine articles: lead paragraph, nut graph (explained below), point one, point two, etc., the end.

In chapter 2 of this book, we mentioned the nut graph, a paragraph (or a sentence) in your story that distills its essence. The nut graph comes after your lead; it is comparable to a thesis statement in an essay, if you still remember high-school English class. Consider this article by Stephanie on "spiritual journeying," a national trend in tourism that has implications for New Mexico businesses. Here's the lead:

> Ever since the Beatles met the Maharishi, the phrase "spiritual journeying" has taken on literal dimensions. Getting in touch with a higher power can be a real trip, thanks to retreat centers that are cashing in on the religious and meditative interests of the alternative tourist crowd.

Now, here's the "nut," which came in the next paragraph:

> The Land of Enchantment is a true believer in the economic value of waylaying travelers on the path to enlightenment.

And that's what the article is about—not the national trend, but how New Mexico's Tourism Department is leveraging that trend to attract vacation travelers.

You might want to use more than one sentence to describe the gist of your article. Your nut graph might summarize all of the important points you are going to bring out, as in this example from Emily's article on how to return to a more holistic way of eating, published in *Conscious Choice*.

The point she makes in her lead tells how dangerous it is that Americans have become consumers of processed foods.

> Dangerous, perhaps, because the links in the food chain have gotten a lot longer. Back before the invention of the modern food industry, we ate what we grew. It was as simple as that. These days, our food travels from pesticide-laden industrial farm, to processor, to packager, to trucking facility, to warehouse, to supermarket. Along the way, various harmful wastes are added to our food which ultimately result in environmental degradation—and our own. They range from pesticide residues to industrial waste, to the use of and later the emission of fossil fuels, to packaging tossed in the landfill.

She goes on to untangle and explain all of those practices and show how they affect the quality of the food we eat—even describing whether or not it is really "food."

Practice writing the one-sentence and one-paragraph versions of your nut graph. If you are having trouble condensing your idea or slant, you probably need to conduct more research or interviews before you continue writing the article. If you can nail down the slant of your story, continue writing the middle section.

Shaping Up

Here's a sample outline for an article about when to use your personal credit card for business expenses:

Lead: "Common wisdom tells you *never* to use your personal credit cards to provide funds for the business you own. High interest rates make using credit cards seem like an expensive way to get capital, and it's not a good idea to mix business and personal finances. Right?" (Using the "Ask a Question" technique, see page 62).

Nut Graph: "Well, most of the time. However, every business owner knows there are occasions that call for the judicious use of a credit card to provide working capital."

Point 1: Here are all the bankers' warnings, and tips from a real banker:
—When you mix consumer and business transactions, it's hard to demonstrate the business's creditworthiness when it's time to get a loan.
—It's a good idea to apply for a separate credit card for business expenses only.
—Business credit cards can offer certain perks valuable to business owners.

Point 2: Here are the three times when using a personal credit card can be helpful (with more warnings):
—You can't get a loan by any other means.
—You need cash on a short-term basis only.
—You encounter a deal you just can't pass up.

Ending: "I would suggest that these are the *only* exceptions to the rule." (Using the "Apt Quote" method, see page 62.)

Sidebar (which would have interrupted the story flow if it had been placed in the main body of the article): According to credible statistics, women business owners are using credit cards more often than men to fund their businesses.

After nailing the nut graph, you will go on to list the important points in your story, usually in descending order of importance. That way, if your busy reader stops reading halfway through, he or she will at least have assimilated the main facts you wish to impart. This technique, called pyramid style, was the basic structure used by newspaper reporters before electronic publishing came along. If their editors had to shorten an article to fit space requirements, they simply cut from the bottom, confident that the important points would not be lost. You can still use pyramid style as the basic organizing structure for your articles.

Sometimes the main points of your story are delineated by subheadings, much like the sections in this book. For an article on family-owned businesses and succession planning, Stephanie gleaned three major points from her expert interviewees: that family-owned businesses need a buy-sell agreement in place before the founder retires, dies, or becomes disabled; that the cash needs of family-owned business founders differ with disability and retirement; and that grooming a successor is an important part of the plan. Those three salient points became subheadings in a 2,000-word article on the subject. Within those headings, each subtopic had its own points, creating a rich structure for this how-to feature.

In a smaller piece, like a 1,000-word article, you will have a lead, an ending, and two or three points in between in which to inform the reader. Use that simple format—lead, point 1, point 2, point 3, and the conclusion—as the structure behind your 1,000-word article. Each paragraph will be about two hundred words long. Breaking this article down into it simplest components is the easiest way to explicate your ideas.

Here's an insider 's tip: even if you don't include them in your final submission, you might want to write subheads just to keep your points organized. Then delete them, and write a transition between paragraphs.

You can write a five-paragraph article by flipping the pyramid upside down—starting with the less important stuff (the bottom of the pyramid) and gradually building momentum to a surprising ending (the point of the pyramid, and of your story). This technique can be used to lend "punch" to a story when to state the most important point first would cause its impact to fizzle.

Other types of articles—the personal column or the department piece—will be more linear in form simply because they are shorter. By linear, we mean that these will contain a one-point argument with facts to back it up. Your facts become the individual points in this format, supporting the one main point of which you want to persuade the reader. Here's a well-known example:

> Virginia, your little friends are wrong. They have been affected by the skepticism of a skeptical age. They do not believe except what they see. They think that nothing can be which is not comprehensible by their little minds. All minds, Virginia, whether they be men's or children's, are little. In this great universe of ours, man is a mere insect, an ant, in his intellect as compared with the boundless world about him, as measured by the intelligence capable of grasping the whole of truth and knowledge.
>
> Yes, Virginia, there is a Santa Claus. . . .

This famous editorial by Francis Pharcellus Church of the *New York Sun* goes on to list all of the points that he believes prove the existence of Santa Claus. Santa Claus exists, just as "love and generosity and devotion exist." The world would be "dreary" without him. There's no proof that he doesn't exist. People who believe in "faith, poetry, love and romance" can see that he lives. And he will live forever.

This short piece, written in response to Virginia O'Hanlon's letter to the editor, had one major point: there is a Santa Claus. The editor's "proof" consisted of individual beliefs, or points, building toward a powerful ending: not only does he live now, but there will always be a Santa Claus. Think of the linear format of a short column or opinion essay as an arrow that makes a straight shot to the conclusion.

The middle section of your article should have a flow that keeps the reader reading. Link paragraph to paragraph to hold reader interest and establish a smooth transition from one idea to the next.

The easiest way to link paragraphs is with words that repeat a phrase or an idea. Here is an excerpt from a book review, written by Stephanie, of a biography of Quanah Parker, the last Comanche chief:

> The author gives equal weight to both sides of this man's remarkable existence, providing a balanced view of the Comanche warrior who became a peaceful Texas rancher.
>
> Part of that balance lies in Neeley's even-handed admiration for warriors in both sides of the conflict. . . .

The repetition of the idea of "balance" in the second paragraph and the use of other words that connote balance—"even-handed" and "both sides"—make a nice transition to the next point.

You will discover your own techniques for smooth transitions. Making one paragraph flow into another is a detail that signals your knowledge of the subject and the care you took in writing the article.

This is a good place to mention sidebars. A sidebar to an article might break out interesting points from the article. It might add information to an article, such as a brief company history or a list of the "Ten most common mistakes new managers make." A sidebar also can elaborate on a point that is relevant to the article, but would have broken up the flow of the story. It's a great place to put a bunch of clunky numbers—such as the company's annual revenues and number of employees. See our sidebar "Shaping Up" (page 59) for an outline of an article that took an interesting but flow-interrupting point 3 and put it in a sidebar instead.

When you take an assignment, be sure to ask your editor if sidebars are included in or separate from the article's word count.

Happy Endings

In writing as in life, endings can be difficult. You've written an interesting lead, built a strong middle based on relevant points, and now you need a memorable conclusion. Here are three techniques that work for us.

End with an Apt Quote or Anecdote

Often, an interviewee will sum up the most important point in an article with a line or a brief story that really says it all.

In an article for a trade journal in the energy industry, Stephanie wrote a feature about how slow the southeastern states were to adopt electric utility restructuring compared to the rest of the country. The conclusion was that, although they were taking their time, electricity deregulation in these states was inevitable. One of the experts summed up: "Everybody understands that, at one time, we were doubting that competition was going to come. I don't think we doubt it anymore." That concession concluded the article.

Circle Around

Tease something out of the beginning or body of your article and end with a reference to it. A circular structure is very satisfying to write and to read.

Emily's article for *BusinessWeek's* international edition on "Santa Fe's High-Tech Chaparral" talked about the early days of a now-successful high-tech incubator that initially had trouble attracting members and had no fixed venue to meet. "It even, for a time, landed far out of town at the grim Santa Fe Airport cafeteria." Later in the article, she writes that the group is still rootless, but now it's because they are so popular that they can't find a place big enough to hold their meetings. She ends the article with "Airport cafeterias need not apply," providing a humorous and meaningful ending.

In an article for a Connecticut community newspaper, Stephanie wrote about a psychic who had developed a system of numerology to define certain characteristics of people in love. The psychic based this system of "Love Numbers" on a calculation involving a person's birth date—like the signs of the zodiac—each number from one to nine having assigned personality traits. The article began: "At 'sixes and sevens' in your love life?" Stephanie ended the piece by asking the psychic to explain how a six and a seven might fare together in a love relationship.

Intrigue the Reader with a New Fact

"By the time you wrap your fish in this article, however, things might have changed. (And here's why)." This is one of our favorite ways to end an article. If you can give your reader a fresh new angle to noodle around, he or she will anticipate your next article on the subject.

You may simply end your article with a call to action, as in: "As you write them, keep a list of your own techniques for ending an article in a satisfying manner."

Cleaning House

One of our expert interviewees for this book informed us that she never hires business people to write articles because they generally are such poor writers.

We don't quite agree. We know you know how to write. We know you write every day, and that most of the writing you do is business writing. The goal of business writing is to communicate quickly and clearly.

The goal of writing about business, however, is to impart useful information accurately and with style. Because your daily business writing is fast and to the point, you might have forgotten about style. Because you work in an industry where shorthand gets to the point quicker, your written words may be filled with jargon and acronyms that are meaningless to people other than your colleagues. And because it's been a long time since elementary school, you might have forgotten some of the finer points of grammar.

We are not going to become your English teachers. But we would like to point out a few of the most common writing mistakes made by business people. In our experience, these are the errors that can bring your writing down several notches. They also signal "beginner" to any editor. Think of this section as a housekeeping lesson, with tips and tricks to help you clean up your writing before you show it around.

Beginning at the Beginning

As we mentioned in the section on leads, the story you are writing doesn't start at the beginning. It begins in the present-day, with the current news or trend or event, and goes on from there. No busy reader is going to slog through the history of mechanical engineering (or even just one engineering firm) to get to the point. Put any *back story*—relevant details the reader must know to understand the whole story—farther down in your middle section. Keep history out of your lead.

Hiding the Nut

You know what your story is about, but you must communicate that content to the reader early in the text. A clear statement of content—"Every business owner knows there are occasions that call for the judicious use of a credit card to provide working capital"—tells the reader what the article is going to be about. Never bury your nut graph.

Burying the Lead

Hiding the nut's best friend. Often, inexperienced writers begin a story with a wandering and uninteresting lead, but in paragraph six, there's an anecdote, quote, or detail that would have made an ideal lead. Sometimes editors call this "warm up" and many writers do it. The way to avoid this is to read your story out loud. Do you begin with something interesting? Or is the best stuff way at the bottom? If so, then you know you hid the nut and buried the lead.

Leaving out the Basics

You may not be writing a news story, but there is an enormous amount of reportage in any business article you will write. If you are writing about a company, your readers will want to know when that company was established, how many employees it has, where it is located, what its annual revenues are, and which other companies are its competitors. Even if you put this information in a sidebar, it's still vital to the story. See our sidebar "Twenty-five Questions to Ask Any Business" (pages 46–7), that will keep you from overlooking the obvious in an interview. Get the answers to the basic questions first. Double-check the spelling of all proper nouns.

Crafting One-Sided Pieces

If you want to write press releases, go into public relations. Objectivity and balance are the hallmarks of good writing for publication. If the issue is controversial, you have an obligation to report what the other side has to say. If a company has close competitors, your article will be more complete if you talk to them as well. Don't rely on one source to get the whole story. Stylistically, curb superlatives, like "world's greatest" or "largest ever," unless you can back them up with facts.

Using Jargon and Acronyms without Explanation

Jargon and acronyms are shorthand expressions used by people who say the same things over and over. It's easier to say "carrier" than "insurance company." It's faster to say "OSHA" than "Occupational Safety & Health Administration." Everyone uses jargon and acronyms within their fields, when with colleagues. When you write for a wider audience, however, it's only polite to explain yourself. While editing your article, be sure that all such terms are defined clearly for your audience.

Writing in the Passive Voice

If the subject takes action, your sentence will be stronger. "The company posted third-quarter results," not "Third-quarter results were posted by the company." Whenever you have "by" in a sentence—"The meeting was held by City Council"—it's a clue that you may be writing in the passive voice. "City Council held the meeting" is a much more decisive construction. Passive voice weakens your writing. Write in the active voice.

Not Varying Sentence Structure

We have all read articles from the "See Dick run. Run, Dick, run" school of writing. As you are writing, stop and read your story aloud to get a sense of its rhythm. If there are too many sentences that scan exactly the same way, join two into a complex sentence or rewrite others. Short, declarative sentences are fine, if you vary them with complex or connected sentences.

Please see the appendix of this book (pages 125–6) for a list of our favorite reference books for style and usage.

To Do Today

- ☐ Read sample articles like the one you will be writing. Analyze their structures.
- ☐ Write your lead in each of the five techniques we suggest, then choose the most engaging one.
- ☐ Look over your research and interview notes and write your nut graph. See if you can fit it on the back of a standard-size business card.
- ☐ Outline your article's major points; write the middle section.
- ☐ Look over our three techniques for ending a story; write your ending three different ways, then choose the strongest one.

Interview with Marc Ballon,

who has been a writer for thirteen years. He has covered business for the *Los Angeles Times* and has been a staff writer at both *Inc.* magazine and *Forbes.* His freelance work has appeared in *The Christian Science Monitor, U.S. News and World Report, The Baltimore Sun,* and *The San Francisco Chronicle,* among others. He's currently a staff writer at the *Jewish Journal of Greater Los Angeles.*

Which questions about structure and format must a writer ask of the editor upon receiving an assignment?

I would want to know exactly what the focus of the story is. Whatever the editor says is the focus is what I would lead with, and I would work backwards from there. The type of story would inform the structure. For example, if it were a hard news story, I'd be more inclined to go with news at the beginning of the story. If it were a feature, I'd start with an anecdotal lead, and work my way into it. If it were a service piece, I'd have a couple of paragraphs of introduction, and background, and then have some bullet points after that. It helps me if the editor gives me a list of questions before I delve into it. If the editor says, "We want to know when it happened, why it happened, is it an isolated event or part of a bigger trend," then all those questions will be part of the story. So the editor is really giving you an outline.

Do you outline? What are your favorite techniques for keeping yourself going from lead to conclusion?

I don't outline formally, but I'll outline in my head, or I'll jot down a few topic sentences and ideas on a piece of paper and then get started. If I'm pressed for time, I will even sit down after I've done some background research and had a conversation with the editor and actually write out a story. Then I'll see where the holes are and fill in the holes with more reporting. If I have a lot of time, I will write out a formal outline, and the outline sometimes serves as a first draft, with topic sentences that just go on and on. That outline is my first draft. That's the foundation for the story. Sometimes I'll write on the top of my outline a series of questions I want to have answered, so when I talk to people I have a clear direction.

While a writer is hammering a story into a structure, that writer must be certain that he or she is not also "leading" the story to fit a preconceived idea. How does a writer "follow" the story?

Sometimes I write the story first, and if my reporting reveals other truths or nuances, I'll go back in and revise it. I'm constantly revising. Just having something on the page gives me confidence, and that's a writer's best friend.

Without good structure, you cannot write a good story. It's the foundation for a strong, compelling narrative.◆

6. Shrink Your Business, Make More Money

A funny thing happened on the way to our writing careers: we became specialists almost without our noticing it. And if we'd known how to focus our industry and business knowledge to launch and nurture our careers, we would have made more money, sooner. We hope to help you skip the trial-and-error period and go straight to more efficient ways of working as a writer.

Part of our business lexicon for decades, *niche marketing* means the process of selling a unique product or service to a specific group of potential customers. In a way, this entire book is about niche marketing. We are advising you to specialize in the field in which you now work. Now, within that field, we can help you zero in on just a few topics that will strengthen your writing and bring you more work.

Think of the businesses you know that are focused on niches (just about every one is nowadays). An article in the *Boston Business Journal* last year detailed law firms that cater to highly paid executives who are leaving their companies or starting new jobs. The law firms had specialists who could draw up employment contracts, negotiate severance and exit pay, and even come up with family trusts for the well-paid executives.

Although the firms mentioned in the article fell under the category of corporate law firms, each one had certain attorneys who concentrated only on employment law—and commanded a higher wage for their work. Once these individuals developed their specialties, their clients referred other executives looking for similar services. The time they spent on developing new business diminished, while they were able to make more money for the firm, and offer specialized service to a select group of people.

Now, think about the businesses that try to be all things to all people: they often fail to differentiate themselves from similar businesses in the same category. In your neighborhood, you'll likely find one intersection with a gas station on every corner. Gas prices may differ by a penny, but that's not enough to make a dangerous left turn worthwhile. Your gas purchasing decision is based purely on which corner gas station happens to be most convenient. Not surprisingly, running a gas station is a low-profit, low-margin business, based on volume. That means gas stations need to serve as many people as possible because they make only pennies on each sale.

For writers, just as for the lawyers at those Boston law firms, building a strong niche can mean the difference between turning out high-quality work for select, well-paying clients, and being run ragged churning out a huge variety of stories for low pay. You want to be a high-paid specialist (employment lawyer), not a pennies-earning generalist (the corner gas station).

How Do You Find Your Niche?

For some writers, specialization develops by accident, while others actively cultivate their niches. For Dawne Shand, a freelance writer based in Newburyport, Massachusetts, her niche marketing began when she worked on a research project in her management-consulting job. After turning in a rewrite of a client's project, "suddenly the [client's] editors were saying, 'You have a nice writing style. Would you like to write for us?'" Shand recounts. She then began freelancing more seriously, writing for *Knowledge Management*, a computer trade magazine. "My expertise in the field was the primary reason they assigned stories to me, and more importantly, why they overlooked my flaws as a writer of feature length stories."

Emily started her career as a generalist. She took work from whomever would give it to her, from political articles for the alternative weekly newspaper, to a series on historic Denver neighborhoods for a glossy city magazine. Although her early career looked scattered at first, a pattern eventually emerged.

One of Emily's first full-length magazine stories was about the difficulties of exporting for small businesses. She'd recently graduated from the University of Denver's international management MBA program, where she'd been writing academic papers about international trade. After interning with the Department of Commerce's international trade division, Emily had worked directly with several area small businesses interested in exporting. She knew the names of people with interesting stories to tell before she pitched to the editor. In fact, the idea for the article had been germinating for some time. The magazine that bought her story, *Colorado Business*, became a regular customer.

In the meantime, Emily, desperate to make a living as a writer, took any freelance job that came her way. Often she'd find herself interviewing ten unrelated people for four or five articles on different topics. It was chaotic.

Despite efforts to thwart her niche from developing, the work for *Colorado Business* lead to an interview for the *Boulder Daily Camera*'s weekly business insert, "Business Plus." She showed the editor her clips, all related to business, and landed a regular assignment writing weekly small business profiles. Her business-writing niche was coming into focus.

Through networking, Emily then landed a freelance job for *Natural Foods Merchandiser*, a national trade publication published in Boulder. She wrote service articles on running different aspects of retail stores. In the meantime, she was developing a Rolodex full of names of experts on small business, a list of inside sources, and a file-folder of possible story ideas, all related to her work with small business. In a secondary niche, she wrote about the business of retailing natural foods. Although she didn't wake up one morning and say, "I'm going to write about business," it became clear that's where her strength lay as a writer.

Gradually, her work pared down to a manageable level, largely because she became focused on two niches. She ditched the alternative weekly and the city magazine. Instead, she focused on two lucrative clients, *Colorado Business* and *Natural Foods Merchandiser*. Within the two categories of small business and natural foods retailing, she wrote on technology, merchandising, demographics, human resources, and myriad other topics. She spent less time prospecting for stories or desperately trying to find sources for topics she knew nothing about. Instead, research for each article lead to a list of ideas for other articles, ones that she could easily pitch. While Emily's specialization did become business journalism, she developed the ability to write on a variety of topics within that niche.

Subject matter is not the only way to define your niche. The form your writing takes can be a specialty, too. For example, Stephanie is also a freelance business journalist. Under that designation, she is a real generalist. She writes about energy, venture capitalists, minority-owned businesses, tourism, biotechnology, and a host of other topics. Anything the editors want her to tackle, she's game.

However, the articles that Stephanie writes are mainly feature articles. They discuss trends, not hard news. Most feature articles are tied to a news hook—think about all of the features discussing matters related to the events of September 11 in the various areas of national security, human rights, the historical context, and other subject fields. But features are not news reportage in themselves. A feature article has a very specific slant and can discuss the implications of a newsworthy event, rather than simply report on the event itself.

Stephanie specializes by creating niches that are about format, not subject (see chapter 2, "What the Market Will Bear," for more on the types of articles that editors will buy). She thinks of the article formats she offers as products on a shelf. Within her business writing, she sells feature articles and profiles of people and their businesses. Within her garden-writing for gardening magazines and publishers, she writes columns and books. That's it. She doesn't write news items or promotional materials. Editors know her as a feature and profile writer, and hire her for that specific work. Paring down the types of articles she writes has helped Stephanie polish her form, generate more ideas, and find more work.

Using Your Body of Knowledge

Has anyone ever said to you, "Gee, you know a lot about ___(insert topic here)?" We're certain that if you thought about it, you could come up with a long list of topics you know something about. Writing about those things will be the most efficient way for you to cultivate a thriving writing career. We're talking about basic business tenets here: efficiency, effectiveness, and turning out quality work in the least amount of time.

Consider all the topics you can write about in just one small area. Emily, spinning off her job as a newspaper editor, is able to write about coaching writers, surviving an acquisition, executing a newspaper redesign, planning a feature story, editing, and scores of other topics having to do with running a weekly business paper. On a more personal level, she can also write about small farm management, yoga for horseback riders, integrating new horses into the herd, and other topics related to caring for and riding dressage horses. While this seems like an array of topics, really they all fall under two categories: newspaper business and horses.

Shand says her expertise in knowledge management, an esoteric field that was all the rage when she was starting out, did get her started as a writer. "But had I limited myself to that field, I would have starved," she says. In addition, Shand broadened her niche to include emerging business and technology trends. She markets herself as a business technology trend spotter, and has built a reputation in that field. "Keep in mind," she adds, "interest in content areas only lasts so long. Magazines are fickle beasts."

Let's say you manage a retail store. Your previous magazine research likely revealed a variety of trade magazines—many with seemingly similar missions—within the category "trade magazines for retailers." But each will have a different slant. You could, if your niche is retailing, write for any of the many titles in this category, including *College Store*, *Kitchenware News*, *Party and Paper Retailer*, or *Store Equipment and Design*. Spin your niche a bit differently, and you'll open other doors. You could, for example, write an insider's article on how to find the best sales at your favorite stores, offering up such tips as when retailers generally start to discount inventory prior to the new season. An article like that could sell to women's, teen, or household magazines. But it is still in the retail category.

Think about your life right now. You have a job, which you've learned to do well. Whether it's managing a multimillion-dollar company or running your own small shop, you have specific and detailed knowledge about your work, your industry, and the satellite industries that serve your business. In addition to this broad knowledge, perhaps you have special skills—you know how to talk to irate customers, or are particularly skilled with a certain aspect of accounting. This is all fodder for articles.

You've already taken the time to learn about what you do, and to come up with ideas to improve your business. You read trade journals, attend conferences where speakers discuss industry trends. You've read books on your business, and you know who studies your industry. In short, you know who the players are, which companies dominate, and who everyone turns to for advice. You can easily outline various trends and issues facing the industry.

Now make a list: Write the name of your industry at the top of the page. Then write your job title, and below it write a list of daily tasks. Include even the most mundane parts of your job. It's specific details about surprising things that make writing great. Also write a list of other elements you may know about your business, such as industry trends, vendor concerns, and labor issues.

Write a similar list of hobbies, and list any specialized knowledge you or your acquaintances may have. Kelly James Enger's list, which appeared in *The Writer* magazine in an article about finding your writing niche, included "My father is a dentist" and "My sister is a police officer," in addition to the entries on herself, "Lawyer" and "Vegetarian." Don't leave anything out—you'll find sources for articles in every corner of your life.

For now, pick two or three things you really know a lot about. It's okay to branch out later when you've got a solid niche built. For now, though, think of your career as a young tree with a thin trunk. Your business or industry knowledge is that trunk, and each story you write adds a layer to it, with it gradually growing thicker and sprouting branches. Each subniche you add, or subspecialty, is a branch stretching from that trunk.

Say your business, like Emily's, is running a weekly newspaper. "Newspaper management" may be your trunk, while elements of newspaper management, such as budgeting, assigning stories to freelancers, and managing a classified sales staff, are branches coming off the tree.

Maybe the tree has a small offshoot, and that's your hobby writing. Stephanie writes about small business as her primary beat, but also writes gardening books and articles. Emily also writes about business, but has a small equestrian magazine niche. Generally, your business niche will sustain you financially and your hobby writing will propagate your slush fund.

Concentrate your writing efforts on this one trunk. As the tree matures, it will grow new branches, and as your career grows, it too will sprout surprising offshoots. Most writers will tell you the process of growing a career is organic: you start with one thing and somehow end up writing about related topics over the course of time. Sometimes those surprising assignments turn into much larger trees of their own. You may end up with three trees growing in your writing garden. That's okay—you just don't want to end up managing a whole forest.

Efficiency as a Game Plan

Why is developing a niche so important? As the editor of a business weekly, Emily notes that it takes a new reporter learning a beat about six months to find his or her sources, understand the nuances of the industry he or she covers, track the trends over time, and write knowledgeably about a topic. But as a writer with specific knowledge, you're several steps up on a platform of knowledge. No arduous climbing for you. You'll use each interview and research session to

Hot Business Beats

1. Industries in turmoil. Think about the uncertainty of the post-September 11 airline industry; the chaos of state-by-state utilities deregulation; insurance companies getting out of the business rather than writing medical malpractice policies. Any industry undergoing a transformation is a prime topic for editors. If you can explain those changes and their implications—for the players, for their customers, for the economy—you are a valuable writer to a business editor.
2. Lifestyle industries. Americans love their stuff. If you're in the retail business or design and/or manufacture sporting goods, or are in another goods-related field, you're in a unique position to write about trends and practices. Depending on your slant, professionals in your field, and even your consumers themselves, will read what you write.
3. Technology for the masses. Can you write clearly about complex scientific or technological topics? Are you an engineer with a sense of poetry and clarity? Editors want to hear from you. Magazines and newspapers are always looking for trend stories on the latest and greatest technological innovation that will to revolutionize business. They can't always find writers who can explain these subjects clearly. Science and technology writers are always in high demand.
4. Healthcare. Baby boomers, the largest demographic segment of the population, are aging; the healthcare system is in turmoil (see number 1), and seeing a doctor can be an incredibly complex and frightening task these days. If you understand the healthcare system and can write about it clearly and intelligently you'll have plenty of work. This is one of those niches that touches everyone—engineers, storeowners, mothers, and construction workers all want to understand the healthcare system.

5. Biotech and biomedical fields. Relatively unknown a decade ago, biotechnology and biomedical information is coming into the mainstream. Can you write about new inventions or the newly emerging biotechnology business segment? Do you know insiders who can point you to the newest trends? If so, editors will keep you busy writing about these hot topics.

spin off new ideas, and writing within one industry allows you to know a lot of different people, both sources and editors, all in the same category.

Every time a writer researches an article and interviews a source, he or she is adding to him or her portfolio of knowledge and his or her Rolodex of sources. You'll fill a file-folder of notes, but you'll use only about 20 percent of the accumulated information. The rest, well, think of it as an idea receptacle. From it, you can pluck an idea and grow it into yet another story. And that's how niches are born.

A few years ago, everyone in the utilities industry was talking about deregulation. Although many people had read about it in the newspaper, the actual ins and outs of taking a regulated utility such as electric service and privatizing it was vastly complex. Although Emily wasn't a utilities expert, she did a story for *Inc.* magazine on a company that planned to take advantage of deregulation to market "green," or environmentally friendly, energy. It took her a long time to really understand the complexities; but once she did, she went on to write several additional articles on the topic.

While she was trying to learn about Green Mountain Energy Company, one of her sources mentioned a company that had developed an Internet site that could make instant energy trades (an Enron competitor). She later wrote another piece on that company.

Not only can nuggets be pulled from stories to develop other stories, but one story, with all that information you've collected, can be spun to sell to a variety of different publications.

Let's say that Emily decides to write "Surviving an Acquisition" as a personal-experience piece (her newspaper was sold to American City Business Journals, their forty-second acquisition). She could sell it to journalism trade publications because other editors and writers might be interested in reading about her experience. She could rewrite the piece in a more general fashion, add an interview or two, and resell it to a general business magazine. She could write the piece as a service, or how-to article, and once again a new audience is waiting. The story could sell to writing magazines, business magazines, and trade magazines for the publishing industry, all within the same niche.

And because you've got a Rolodex of sources, each recasting of the article requires just a quick scan through to find a few new voices who can add insight to the piece for a particular angle. As you get to know the stable of editors who look for work in your industry, you'll know exactly what each is looking for and can spend less time figuring out who's who and what they want. You can mine a deep body of knowledge to include different information for different editors. That's why developing a strong niche is so important: every article leads to more work, in a specific field.

Speaking the Language

Another reason to focus on a niche: your insider's knowledge of your business means you know much more than the average person. You learn about innovations, trends, and other elements long before the general public, and even before many in your industry. You speak the language. You understand the industry's hot buttons, and can impress editors with your knowledge of the subject matter by hitting on exactly what people in the industry are talking about.

For example, suppose your officemates are talking about a great new technology and how it will change business practices in your industry. Although the editor of your industry's main trade journal may know about the technology, he may not know all its applications. In addition, you could pitch this same story to a national business magazine that might not even be aware of the technology.

Beware of jargon, however. This is a common downfall of writers who know so much about a subject they assume the audience does as well, or their minds are garbled with language that may mean something to insiders, but means nothing to readers. There's a fine line between speaking the language and writing superficially. So, while you'll be able to pitch to an editor with a strong insider's idea, make sure you write it clearly and without industry jargon (see chapter 5, "Building a Strong Structure," for more about how to rid your writing of industry slang).

A Million Stories in One Room

Remember the trade show you went to in Des Moines? Or was it Chicago? Remember sitting through a boring speech about some topic related to your industry? Or maybe you're headed to the annual conference this year. Make your attendance more productive. Attend the sessions, meet the speakers, and read the bios. Who specializes in what areas of your industry? What topics appear to be of interest to the participants and attendees of the conference? You're mining the trade show or conference experience for writing material.

Industry conferences and trade shows, as we mentioned in chapter 2, are great places for writers to network. You'll find a whole world of possible sources, all in one hotel conference center. Vendors to your industry, experts who give speeches, lead workshops or simply pay attention to the industry, can all be sources for stories in the future. And they're all there in one giant, brightly lit convention center. Work the room, collect business cards, talk to as many people as you can. Each one could be useful to you now, or in the future.

You'll use all those people as sources for your stories and ways to generate ideas. Write a list of everyone you know in the industry: the speakers at the conferences, the analysts who cover publicly traded companies in your industry, CEOs of your company and your competitors, managers, and vice presidents, people who research product or industry trends. Next to their names, write what you know about them already—maybe they have a cynical take on something; maybe they've invented the next big thing, or have a bizarre hobby. Some of them might make excellent personality profiles, and some of them might turn out to be useful insiders who'll help you get a great story that no one else has written. Some will serve as expert voices in your articles. The point is, because you work in the industry, you'll spend less time looking for appropriate contacts. After a while, you could even call yourself an expert.

More Cash, Less Work

Editors pay attention to bylines. If you're writing repeatedly in one particular area, editors who read those publications will begin to see your name over and over again. Once editors realize you specialize in a subject on which they need articles, they'll call you with assignments. Although you'll be diversifying your client base, you'll still be covering the same niche. And once you've established yourself as a specialist, you can command a slightly higher wage.

Not only will you make more money, but it's almost guaranteed that you'll write better, too. Heard the old adage, "Write what you know?" It definitely applies in this case. Your articles will be much clearer, and more authoritative for the reader, and they'll be much more fun for you to write. And don't stick to just your profession: mine your hobbies, your spouse's hobbies or profession, or take a personal experience you've had and expand it into a niche.

It's the Pareto principle, the old 80/20 rule that you probably know from business: 20 percent of your customers make up 80 percent of your sales. The same is true for writing: you need to dig out your niche, mine it for good customers and good ideas. The rest is gravy.

So, if you concentrate on writing what you know, you've got the contacts, you've got the knowledge. Now all you have to do is develop the stories.

To Do Today

- ☐ On a piece of paper, write down your industry name, job title, and job duties. Be specific—don't just write "accounting"—write "accounting for publicly traded companies," for example.
- ☐ Create a list of people you know; be thorough. Include speakers you've seen at conferences and people you haven't yet met in person, but who are experts in the field.
- ☐ Network with writers already working in your niche. Find their bylines in trade magazines and set up informational interviews with them. Grill them on industry trends (but don't steal their ideas, use them for educational purposes only).

Interview with Rene Jackson,

a registered nurse in Port Charlotte, Florida, began writing for nursing trade publications about two years ago. Her goal is to write full time. Rene says that after gaining experience in, and being comfortable with, nursing, writing seemed a logical extension.

How did your niche evolve? Did you decide (consciously) to write about nursing and healthcare from the beginning, or did it just happen?

I started writing what I knew best: nursing and healthcare. About two years ago, I decided to query some nursing magazines and started with *Nursing Spectrum*, which published my first article. I have since written for several nursing magazines, and reviewed for Lippincott, Williams, and Wilkins, a healthcare publishing company.

How did you get your first assignments? Do you write query letters or have you developed a regular clientele? If so, how did that happen?

Nursing Spectrum also published my second article on cruise nursing. I write frequently for several nursing magazines, by both submitting ideas and accepting assignments. I also write small 200-word articles related to teen healthcare, for *Master Teacher*. They publish newsletters for educators.

Has being a professional in the healthcare industry helped you land writing jobs?

Definitely. I write from personal experience, though I like writing clinical articles less than I do those having to do with such topics as ethics, nursing law, and other current healthcare issues. I pretty much accept all assignments at this stage of my writing career, because it gives me experience, and in doing the research on particular topics, I expand my knowledge base. For instance, for *Advance for Nursing* magazine, I recently did a series of articles on locations [with]in Florida that nurses and their families can relocate to, from [their present Florida locations]. I believe when an editor likes your work ethic (e.g., submitting on time), they will seek you out for future assignments.

Are healthcare writers in demand? Why? What advantages do you have over someone without your professional experience when it comes to writing jobs?

From what I have learned, healthcare writers are in great demand, at all different levels—from simple articles, to grant writing (a specialty), to writing for pharmaceutical companies. The professional experience probably gives me advantages with regard to nursing, but there are many excellent writers, who are not medical personnel, who have been writing about healthcare for many years.◆

7.

Working It

Having followed the "To Do Today" activities in this book, you have introduced yourself to a few editors, analyzed your business-writing market, and hooked your first assignment. You have learned to research efficiently, interview effectively, and focus on a niche, or three, to garner more assignments, more easily.

If you've had some success publishing your work thus far, you might be thinking of pursuing a part-time or full-time writing career. Publishing your articles part-time might be a pleasant way to supplement your income, whether you're still working in your industry or retired from it. On the other hand, you may be considering the full-time writing options available to you.

To give you the flavor of a writer's day, in this chapter we describe the typical duties and schedules of a staff writer, a business editor, and a full-time freelance writer. We also suggest careers for writers that may involve a lot of writing but require other skills as well. Read on to see if one of these full-time jobs could be tailored to fit your dreams.

If you want to publish an occasional article while working in your industry, or write part time, skip on to chapter 9, "Journalistically Speaking," to find out how to strengthen and supplement your writing with speaking and teaching. Or go directly to chapter 10, "Writers Are People Who Write," to find out how to put the polish on your image as a professional writer.

Staff Writer for a Daily Newspaper

Diane Velasco is a former high-school English teacher and business owner who is now a staff reporter for the *Albuquerque Journal*, a daily newspaper. There are two reasons, she says, that she loves to write for a news organization: service to the community and the thrill of the chase. "A staff writer's day is chaotic, deadline driven, fast-paced," Velasco says. "While not every day is like that, you have to be prepared for whatever happens. For me, it was an adjustment working on a daily newspaper because you have to have the confidence and skills to turn a story quickly and accurately. There's no time for writer's block and fussiness. You also have to have the versatility to handle whatever your editor throws at you and deliver it when he or she wants it—or earlier."

Diane is in a unique position to weigh the ups and downs of a staff writer's day: she was the editor of a small community newspaper and a freelance writer before joining the *Journal*. She thinks that being a staff reporter is more fun than "herding cats"—directing reporters—and not nearly as much fun as chasing stories. As a freelance writer, she focused on writing one story at a time, while continually pitching new ideas for articles to keep the money coming in steadily.

The busy day of a staff reporter suits Diane best. "I once covered an all-day bankruptcy hearing where the judge made a final decision about a company," she recalls. "I took notes about dramatic testimony and facts all day long. But the judge didn't make his final decision until 5:00 P.M., and I had a 6:00 P.M. deadline. I raced back to the newsroom and flipped my notebook to the end. I started the story with the judge's decisions and his final words, then filled in the best testimony, facts, and background."

One surprising aspect of staff reporting, Diane says, is the collaborative nature of the newsroom writing process. "Whatever you write, once you submit it, editors and copy editors work it over," she notes. "They reword things, move paragraphs, change leads. Brace yourself for that. Editors will judge your professionalism on how well you accept editing and on how cooperative you are in the process."

Like many business people, a staff writer can look forward to a climb up the ladder, to editor or administrator. Diane sees herself working for a wire news service in the future, or writing for a larger publication so she can focus on international issues.

Editor of a Business Weekly

Emily Esterson is the co-author of this book and, as mentioned previously, is the editor of *New Mexico Business Weekly*, one of the forty-one business weeklies owned by American City Business Journals.

Emily's publication week starts on Friday, at an editorial meeting to plan the next issue, when most of us are winding down the week. "After the staff gives us their stories for the week, we look at what the freelancers are doing," she says. "Then we map the whole thing out, deciding where everything goes."

By early afternoon, Emily has collected a few stories to read through from her edit-in folder. She reads each one at least twice. On the last read-through, she may want to ask the reporter or freelance writer a few questions. The piece may need rewriting. "If it does, I'll really get involved with asking the writer a lot of questions, and may have to move the story to a different place in the newspaper because it wasn't as newsworthy as I thought it would be," she explains. The editor then helps the reporter brainstorm ideas for artwork to accompany the piece, perhaps including charts and graphs, and works with the art director to produce them.

Once the story is *on page*, printed out in its nearly final form, Emily or the managing editor will write the headline and cut the story to fit the space allotted. She then hands the page off to the copy editor for a final editing and proofreading.

This publication schedule is unrelenting through Wednesday night, when the finished newspaper is sent electronically to the printer for a Friday release date. On Thursday, Emily is free to plan the next issue and pending special supplements, answer email, and talk to readers, potential writers, and public-relations professionals who have a story to pitch. "I like Thursday because it's the day I spend prospecting for story leads," she says. "Sometimes I'll search the Web, sometimes I'll go meet people for lunch. Then I feel like I'm really learning about the business community, and what's happening."

Freelance Business Writer

Like a staff writer and an editor, a freelance writer's day is directed by deadlines. Deadlines can overlap, and more than one article must be worked on at one time. So the first priority of the full-time freelance writer is to set up a system to handle the work.

Stephanie Hainsfurther, co-author of this book, is a freelance business journalist. As you have read, she has written for international, national, regional, and local publications on a variety of subjects. Within her business-writing niche she is a generalist, writing on topics as different as tourism and taxes. She keeps drop-in folders and computer files on the topics she writes about most frequently. If she gets an emailed press release from an airline company, for instance, she files it in the computer file marked "Business Travel." If she sees an article on the same subject in the *New York Times*, or a local news item about a business-travel expert, she clips it and drops it in the paper folder. When a business-travel topic comes up for an assignment, Stephanie already has information and ideas for slants at her fingertips.

The texture of a freelancer's day, she says, is determined by the assignments on hand and the writer's flow of energy. "You must do many things besides write," she cautions. "You must sell your work, research, interview, and keep up with your contacts. If you are on deadline, writing becomes the first priority. Do you write first, because you are freshest in the morning? Or do you have to get all of the other stuff out of the way before you can concentrate on your writing? It's good to get into and have a regular schedule."

Stephanie works on as many as eight stories at once. She tries to move each story along each day, paying more attention of course to the ones with closer deadlines. The time in which she must finish a story varies from one week to two months. Her week might begin with eight assignments, all due within the next three weeks, with the first two deadlines on Friday. She might be finishing up interviews for the nearest two; setting up interviews for the next three; and doing preliminary research on three others. How far out from the deadline Stephanie begins work on a story depends on its subject and complexity. "Here's where niche marketing really makes your writing life easier," she states. "If you write regularly about a subject, you can start work closer to the deadline, knowing you have a story and the resources to put it together. The fewer the hours you have to spend on a story, the more money you will make per hour."

Transitions

As a writer, your career track may be more self-directed and less driven by others' expectations than your career in business ever was. The next step may not be as clear as, for example, when a foreman plans to move into an executive position.

A freelance writer, for example, takes assignment after assignment. Certain assignments will present challenges and opportunities—only the freelance writer really knows which ones challenge him or her and which opportunities he or she will want to take. He or she will have to make it up as he or she goes along, a lifestyle that may suit some but not others. Editing is a special talent. An editor might expect a career path that leads into a job as a publisher or administrator, but only if the editor wants, eventually, to get away from editing. A staff writer who enjoys being on the street might or might not take well to a future desk job as an editor.

Taking the plunge may be the only way to find out if you like the work. Some writers break in gradually by moonlighting as freelancers until they can make the switch to full-time writing. Others jump right in. Jacquelyn Lynn, a freelance writer who is our sidebar interviewee for this chapter, quit her job in the motor freight industry when a financial windfall allowed her to write full time. Stephanie borrowed $6,000 from the family savings to quit her job in insurance and set up a newsletter publishing business, only to find out she liked the writing side of the business better than any other part. Emily started out as a freelance writer. Gradually, she learned about different publications, and decided she wanted to work full time as a staff writer, with the goal of moving up to editor. She approached one of her clients, the editor of a food trade magazine, who hired her full time as soon as his budget allowed.

The road to a writing job is as individual as your writing style. As we did in chapter 1, we advise you to network to find available writing jobs. Meet editors and publishers in your community, and don't forget that other published writers are the

Free Online Job Listings for Writers

AssignmentEditor.com
Authorlink.com
Burbages.com/jobs_for_writers.htm
Editorandpublisher.com
Flipdog.com
Freelancewriting.com
Inscriptionsmagazine.com
Journalismjobs.com
Mediabistro.com (International)
Newslink.org
Sunoasis.com
Tjobs.com (jobs for telecommuters)
Writerfind.com
Writerswrite.com/jobs/

best resources. Go to writers' conferences and meet out-of-town editors and publishers and chat with them, even if you don't have anything to pitch. Ask them about job opportunities in general. Some temporary agencies match writers with projects and temporary job opportunities. Online sources of jobs for writers abound, and most are free to the job applicant (see sidebar "Free Online Job Listings for Writers," page 87). Just as you would if you were trying to find another job in your present industry, get a feel for who's hiring and where the jobs are.

Now, all you have to do is figure out which job you want to aim for.

Ten Career Choices for Writers

1. Staff writer. Newspapers and magazines keep writers on staff. Corporations and nonprofits also hire them to work on all kinds of in-house publications, from newsletters to advertising brochures to client proposals.

2. Editor. Ditto. Online publications also employ editors. Publishing houses use editors either on-staff or freelance to copyedit books before they are printed.

3. Freelance writer. Many publications, from international trade magazines to e-zines to your local newspaper hire freelance writers for feature and department writing, critiques and columns.

4. Copywriter/proofreader. Advertising agencies have copywriters on staff to turn out the text for client ad campaigns. Newspapers have staff positions open for copywriters who don't necessarily get a byline, but contribute filler and other regular assignments. Many publications often use copywriters as proofreaders, too.

5. Media liaison. Often called a spokesperson, marketing manager or public-relations representative, the person in this corporate position issues press releases and speaks to reporters. A media representative also would be called upon for policymaking, especially in a crisis situation. At some companies, the titles media liaison, public-relations representative, and communications director might be interchangeable.

6. Communications director. This corporate director might also act as spokesperson, although the duties are broader, encompassing in-house publica-

tions as well as anything that goes out to a client, including advertising, brochures, and proposals.

7. Web content writer/manager. A tech-savvy writer who can manage a website as well as write for it would do well in this varied job.

8. Technical writer. Companies hire specialty writers, like those with knowledge of the high-tech and healthcare fields, to write manuals and other technical materials. Some temporary agencies have expertise in placing technical writers in long-term jobs or project management.

9. Grant writer. Nonprofit organizations especially, like universities, charities, and some hospitals, have a need for people who know where the money is and how to ask for it in writing.

10. Public-relations consultant. Writing is only part of the job when you're in public relations. You have to enjoy lots of face-to-face work with clients. After the press releases are written and placed, you make plenty of telephone calls and office visits to pitch your clients' stories to editors and broadcast news types.

If you're thinking of transitioning to a freelance writing career, read on in chapter 8, "Taking Care of Business," for tips on how to juggle the work and make your billable hours pay more.

To Do Today

- ☐ Write down the pros and cons of a writing career at this time. Weigh your financial options.
- ☐ Meet with other writers, editors, and publishers locally. Talk about the job possibilities and/or the freelance market.
- ☐ Think of a niche you could fill at a local or regional publication. Package it like a product and sell it to them.
- ☐ Sketch out a transition plan to part-time or full-time writing.

Interview with Jacquelyn Lynn,

a prolific, widely published writer specializing in busines, management, and marketing since 1986. Her work has appeared in more than one hundred regional, national, and international publications, including *Entrepreneur* (columnist), *Red Herring, Business Start-ups, Entrepreneur's Home Office, Restaurants USA, Small Business Connection* (published by *Inc.*) and *Commercial Law Bulletin*. Jacquelyn also writes books. Her more recent works include nine books in Entrepreneur Media's business start-up guide series. *How to Start Your Own Business on E-bay* is scheduled for publication in 2004.

Tell us how you got started in your writing career, and how long you've been a freelance writer. Have you written any articles about your former industry?

I have been a freelance writer since 1986. Writing professionally had always been my dream, so that year I decided to take the leap and see if I could make a living as a writer. For the previous ten years, I worked in the transportation industry (air and motor freight) both in operations and in sales/marketing.

I have not written directly about transportation, but have written about sales and marketing, and have used the knowledge I gained about specific industries and general business management in the articles I've written.

Which publications do you write for?

Over the years, my work has been published in more than a hundred local, regional, and national periodicals. I estimate that I've had somewhere in the area of three thousand articles published (a mix of features, shorts, and reprints). My primary periodical market currently is *Entrepreneur*; I have been a columnist for them for thirteen years.

My work tends to go in cycles. For periods, I'll write almost exclusively for magazines, and be writing for fifteen to twenty different publications at the same time. Then I'll shift into more "corporate" work (newsletters, brochures, etc.) for a while. Then get a book contract, then shift back to magazines. For the last several years, I've been writing more books than anything else.

What is the single most important thing you would tell a businessperson who wants to leave his or her industry and become a freelance writer?

Marketing yourself is essential. As a writer, you are a large part of your product. This is a difficult and frustrating business to break into, but if you are a good writer and persistent, you can make it. Understand that this is a business; if you're lucky, you'll spend maybe two-thirds (usually less) of your time researching and writing, and the rest doing administrative work and marketing.

Is there a myth about freelance writing that you'd like to bust?

I don't think it's as much myth as it is misunderstandings and misperceptions. This isn't romantic. With perhaps the exception of a few of the top best-selling novelists, writers don't have full creative control over what they do. We create a product that is a series of written words, and that product has to meet the needs of our customers. The product could be a feature magazine article, a short column, a newsletter, or even a book, but it has to meet the requirements of whomever is paying you to write it, or it will be rejected.

Is it difficult to make a living as a full-time freelance writer? Any tips and tricks on how you supplement that income?

Once I became established as a freelancer (which took about two years), I have never had any trouble making a living. I don't speak or teach, and I consider books part of my freelancing business. I make what I consider to be a comfortable living, I own a home, I don't lack for material things. I probably could make substantially more in sales—but life is too short to spend it doing something you don't enjoy.

Freelancers need to understand basic business, and keep feeding the marketing pipeline even when they are overwhelmed with work. If they don't do that, the work will dry up. I've met many freelancers over the years who just didn't like doing the marketing side, and because of that, couldn't make a living freelancing.

You also have to be comfortable with your income arriving on an erratic basis. Clients and publishers don't pay invoices from writers on a predictable schedule as they do a payroll. I've had to wait for my money from a client or magazine that was having cash flow problems (and once in a great while, you don't get paid at all).

It also helps if you're not snobby about what you write. Not everything you produce is going to be a literary masterpiece. Sometimes you write that instruction manual or sales letter because it's a way to get paid for writing, not because you have a burning desire to write manuals or letters. And these kinds of jobs can lead to others that you'll enjoy better and earn more for.

Is there a question we didn't ask that you'd like to answer?

Be sure you completely understand the terms of your writing contracts, and don't be afraid to change a contract if it's not acceptable.◆

8.

Taking Care of Business

You're a home-based business owner now, whether you're writing and publishing articles full time or part time. There are too few hours in a day and not enough days in the week to allow you to accomplish all the things you have to do. You wear too many hats—president of your company, sales person, administrator, delivery service—to say nothing of all the other people you are—spouse, lover, parent, adult child, amateur athlete, avid reader, you name it—and you feel the pressure. Growing your business right now can seem like an extra burden you don't need, although you may want to grow. We submit that, as a freelance writer, you must develop the business to make those hours pay better.

This chapter is about working smarter, not longer, hours. It contains four different ideas for you. Any one of these methods will expand your writing business today. You can choose just one idea that really works for you, or a combination of two or more, or the whole batch.

Our ideas are meant to work for just about any part- or full-time writer, without a huge outlay of capital. You can use any of these methods without hiring assistants or independent contractors. All techniques are designed for a home-based business owner who is a sole practitioner—perfect for the freelance writer.

1 Trade Up

Because you can't add more hours to your day, you'll have to find a way to make the same hours pay better.

Start by going on a fact-finding mission. You want to determine who your customers are right now, which products or services you provide to which customers, and break those customers down into recognizable categories.

Take out your invoices for the past three months. Make a list, with the name of each major product (feature article, news item, book review, advertorial) or service you sell (writing, public-relations manager, editorial-service provider)—those products and services will be your column headings. Then, make a final column called "customers," and list them. Across the rows, fill in the amount each customer paid for each service over the three-month period (see sidebar on page 95 for a sample chart).

Total the product/service columns. Examine the totals at the bottom of each column, and note the two or three largest amounts. Look at which customers buy which services—and look at what they aren't buying.

Your simple chart will answer three important questions about your business:

1. Which product do I sell the most of, right now?
2. Who buys what I sell?
3. Who buys which services or products?

Use this information to sell more of the top commodities you already provide—to customers you already have.

Let's face it, we're all happy to see our byline appear occasionally, or every month, or every week, in our client publications. Search each publication now for sections you don't write. Eliminate those that are someone else's beat, or column. Look for room to write in areas that are new to you, or in areas that are a natural outgrowth of the type of thing you already write. Once you examine the information you've collected about your company, it's easy to see how each of your existing accounts can be developed. Just sell them the services or products they don't buy now.

Look for offshoots of articles you have already written. It is a far more efficient method of working than tackling a brand new subject every time. The offshoot stories take less time to write—the learning curve is not so steep, after all—and you will be able to mine information from your contacts for a period of time.

Sample "Trading Up" Chart

The following is a sample chart from a freelancer's billing records. The writer now has a clear picture of which types of clients buy which types of writing from her, and how often.

Customers	**Features**	**News**	**Newsletters**	**Ghostwriting**	**Misc.**
Architects, Inc.	—	—	$5,200	$1,200	$500
Insurance Agency	—	—	$5,200	$600	$1,000
Mgmt. Consultants	—	—	$5,200	$1,200	$1,500
Bus. Weekly	$17,000	$5,200	—	—	—
Trade Journal	$9,000	$1,350	—	—	—
National Mag.	$2,400	$3,600	—	—	—
House & Home	$3,000	—	—	—	—
Totals	$31,400	$10,150	$15,600	$3,000	$3,000
Grand Total	$63,150 annually, before taxes and expenses				

Now, let's help this freelance writer analyze the information. Clearly, *Business Weekly* is her anchor client, representing more than 35% of her annual income. Although the freelancer is basically a feature writer for them, she has been successful in spinning off stories from her features that become news items for the paper.

Her corporate clients together represent almost as much of her income as *Business Weekly* does. The first issues of each of the newsletters are time-consuming and labor-intensive. However, subsequent issues are more lucrative when calculated on an hourly basis—they take less time to write, but she makes the same money. Although the ghostwriting and miscellaneous marketing materials she creates for these clients are not a focus, they are essential services that keep the clients happy. She'll not only keep her corporate clients, but will think about adding another newsletter to the mix, a profitable product for her.

The work she does for the trade journal pays more than $10,000 annually and she likes the writing; she is able to spin off some of these features for the *Business Weekly*, as well. No change there.

The national magazine creates far more work in terms of hours spent on research and multiple interviews. It also pays more. The $2,400 figure represents one feature article of 1,800 words; the $3,600 figure represents eight department articles at 600 words each. The feature article was difficult to write and the learning curve was steep; in addition, the editor cannot promise future feature article assignments to this writer at this time. The department articles were easier to write but not of particular subject interest to the writer. This freelancer must make a decision as to whether writing for this national magazine is worth the time, effort, and money.

Writing for the regional "shelter" magazine (*House & Home*) was fun and easy to do. However, it doesn't pay very well. But the writer liked the assignments very much, and is thinking of moving in a new direction with this type of writing. She will continue to write for this publication for practice and published samples, while researching the possibility of making more money on a regular basis with better-paying shelter magazines.

For instance, Stephanie was a freelance feature writer for *New Mexico Business Weekly*. She wrote a feature for the Healthcare Supplement on a privately owned foundation in southern New Mexico that used primates in biomedical research. The USDA had filed charges against the foundation, and it was forced to hand over the chimpanzees it used in experiments to the National Institutes of Health. While covering the matter, Stephanie was in touch with Animal Protection of New Mexico, which subsequently filed a complaint with the New Mexico Pharmaceutical Board against the same foundation for violations in drug dispensing. When they did, Stephanie was a natural to cover it. In fact, Animal Protection gave her a copy of the complaint and the first interview in the matter. She also sold a version of this story to *NMBW*'s regular news pages.

This technique takes far less time, effort, and money than going out and getting brand new customers, or researching new stories for existing customers.

So far, you have pinpointed the things you sell the most of, identified your best customers, and figured out how to develop your existing accounts.

You're working smarter already.

2 Find an Anchor Client

Steady assignments are the backbone of your business. Some business owners call these customers anchor clients. In the same way a shopping mall leases to two or three large anchor stores to bring in a steady stream of customers, your anchors will bring in the bacon no matter what happens in your other accounts. Mary Scott, a freelance writer from Denver, Colorado, writes for finance magazines like *Buyside* and *Research*. She leveraged her insider's knowledge of investments to land an anchor client for whom she researches and writes profiles of analysts. She writes four profiles a month and that work feeds her with material for her other clients. In fact, at this point, Scott only has three clients, makes a great living, and works less than forty hours a week.

One good way to receive routine assignments is to become an outsource for other businesses. Companies of all sizes have laid off many employees, leading them to farm out numerous activities (like the corporate communications functions) to other companies. One of those outsource businesses could be yours.

When Emily was freelancing in Boston, she went looking for an anchor client from whom she'd receive a monthly assignment that would pay a certain portion of her rent. She answered an advertisement in the newspaper looking for a newsletter editor for a publishing company in the management-consulting industry. She interviewed for the full-time job, but convinced the company that they didn't need a full-time editor for this project. Instead, she proposed a scenario where she would freelance the newsletter every month. She got the assignment, and received enough money that she could take on fun, infrequent assignments that maybe didn't pay as well. Later, the company launched a magazine, and she wrote for that as well.

Look back at the records you gathered to help you "trade up." Which products or services do you sell the most? And what types of companies buy them? Go out and sell those same commodities to those same types of companies. While you're at it, remember that you also provide these clients with the following intangibles their in-house personnel don't supply:

— specialized, real-world experience (as opposed to limited, intra-corporate experience)
— up-to-the-minute expertise in your field
— the fast response time only a small company can offer.

When going after anchor clients to offer yourself as an outsource, don't overlook small and medium-sized companies. Smaller companies that can't afford full-time employees need to outsource publications such as newsletters, brochures, and copy for press releases or articles. Small publishing companies are particularly dependent on freelancers to help them at peak times or on short-term projects. They'll hire you again and again for the same type of project or at the same time of year.

For example, *New Mexico Business Weekly* does an annual Santa Fe Business Report. Because it has no reporters in Santa Fe, it must outsource this publication entirely. For three years in a row, the same freelancer got the job. She knew the city and the business community, and she delivered her work on time. Each year, the editor called her with the assignment.

Seven Ways to Waste Your Time

1. Believe fervently in the power of a cold query letter.
2. Decide what you want to write first, then go out and find a market for it.
3. Treat each assignment as a separate story, with no offshoots.
4. Have a lot of small clients that take up as much of your time as one or two larger, better-paying clients.
5. Never stop to analyze your invoice information.
6. Think of other writers merely as rivals, instead of as good sources for more work.
7. Don't share the work when you're swamped.

3 Put Your Business in Its Place

Try to be all things to all people, and you'll find yourself working longer hours for less money. But as savvy businesspeople know, sell just one kind of product or service to one type of customer, and you're likely to find profits rising.

Niche marketing is the simple practice of focusing on what you do best, then targeting those customers who buy that product or service most often (see chapter 6, "Shrink Your Business, Make More Money"). To find your niche and fill it, first examine the competition in your field. Then determine how you provide (or could provide) a product or service that your competitors do not. Remember, you want to claim a particular piece of the market, not the whole enchilada.

Use these three techniques to help your company grow by narrowing its focus:

1. Think small. Offer one thing that gives you an advantage over your competitors. If they are generalists, selling all types of articles to any publication that will buy their work, for example, you could cover just one industry, or topic, or hobby. You're most likely to benefit by filling a need that hasn't been addressed by others.

2. Decide what you do best. If you have special expertise or interest in one area, use it to differentiate yourself from the competition. Your own excitement about and experience in that special area will communicate itself to your editors and readers and help your business flourish.

   For example, if you left a job as an insurance agent to start your own freelance writing business, you have an advantage in writing newsletters for insurance agencies. If you're a former vice president in the food industry, editors might welcome a story about how genetically altered foods are altering the food industry itself. If you're a master gardener, maybe you want to branch out into writing about your hobby and your passion.

   Emily occasionally writes for *Dressage Today*, a horse magazine. She loves the sport and can write passionately about it. The work is easy and enjoyable, and she gets paid to do it. What could be better?

   You get the idea.

3. Find out who your best customers are, and ditch the rest. Again, go back to the information you gathered to "trade up." Who are your largest clients? As mentioned earlier, the famous Pareto principle states that 20 percent of your clients give you 80 percent of your revenue. Why bother with the rest? We'll bet you're spending a lot of time with them for very little return.

4 Promote Your Computer

Can't afford an assistant? Put your computer to work for you. With just three software programs, you can let the machine manage your marketing department. Please make sure all three programs are compatible for easy sharing of data.

1. Use a *list creator* to define and identify your prospects. Many sources offer computerized lists of prospective customers (Dun & Bradstreet's "iMarket, inc." is one good example). You enter certain parameters—company size, location, industry, etc.—to customize a list of companies who buy what you sell.

2. Import that list into your *contact manager*. There are numerous contact-managing software programs on the market; the best have a daily to-do list to

let you know when it's time to call or visit a client or prospect. They also allow you to make dated notes in your customer files to keep track of phone conversations and to schedule future actions to take. They maintain your mailing list and have a mail merge function so you can . . .

3. You can import your contact list into your *word processor* to use these functions. Compose a sales letter or other direct mail piece and send it to the prospects on your list. Your word processing program also should have a mail merge function that allows you to customize your letters with each prospect's name and address, and add an individual's name to the salutation ("Dear Ms. Veep . . . "). With a good word-processing system, printing those individual letters should be a smooth, easy process.

Use the contact manager again to follow up on your mailings with phone calls to those prospects. All three programs work together to provide you with automated marketing assistance, and free you for other important tasks.

Now, get back to work.

To Do Today

- ☐ Make your "Trading Up" chart and analyze your present customer base.
- ☐ Go over materials for articles you're working on right now. Identify offshoots, and pitch them to existing or new customers.
- ☐ Identify one company or publication for which you'd like to write. Figure out how to meet the person who will buy your work.
- ☐ Replace a low-paying client with a higher-paying client.
- ☐ Start using contact-management software that is compatible with your word processing software.

Interview with Stephanie Hainsfurther,

co-author of *Covering the Business Beat,* editor-in-chief of *Albuquerque The Magazine,* and a prolific freelance writer.

To make a living as a freelance writer, you must work on more than one project at a time. How do you maintain your focus when it's time to write?

First of all, I remind myself that there are other things I like about this job besides writing and rewriting. I like to spend quiet time doing research. I like to prepare provocative questions and get to know lots of people by interviewing them. At the right time of day, I even like to catch up on my correspondence and do the "housekeeping" of my business. And I simply can't write for eight to ten hours a day, every day.

Completing one article at a time is not very efficient. I found out long ago that, in order to keep all of my deadlines on track, it really works for me to move each project forward a little at a time. So if I divide my day—say, write for four hours in the morning, when I'm fresh, then set up interviews for most of the afternoon, do a little research before dinner, and return in the evening to organize myself for the next morning—I find I've helped four or five articles toward the finish line, not just one.

Sometimes it really helps to be able to group tasks, which is another good way to work on several articles at once. For instance, I am happiest when I do nothing but interview for a day or three. The ideas have time to gel before I sit down and write those articles.

When it's time to write, I make sure that's all I'm going to do for the prescribed period of time. This is, after all, the most important part of the business, and the one I most enjoy. If I've moved a few projects forward, and now I must write to meet a deadline, I have a clear head for the task. I know that everything else can "cook" while I finish the article at hand.

Publications fold, corporate clients go out of business. When do you find the time to market yourself to new clients?

When I first started out as a freelancer, I couldn't imagine where I'd find the time to keep selling my writing. Just having a handful of clients to please can take up more than forty hours a week. I wouldn't have time to go out and get a new customer until an existing client actually had stopped publishing, or fired me, or went out of business! It was frustrating.

But I'm here to tell you it gets easier. And the reason it does is because of all the people you meet when you're freelancing. Not just the editors and writers with whom you network, but the businesspeople you interview. Their stories multiply. Not all of those stories are suitable for the publications you write for at the moment. You will take some of those stories and place them elsewhere. Your list of clients will grow. More people will tell you more stories. Other writers will refer their surplus stories (and assignments) to you. Editors will think of you when they need an extra article or an interim editor. And you're in business. It really never ends.

How do you keep more than one client happy?

That's probably the easiest part of the job! To me, there are just three things you have to do for all of your editors and corporate clients: challenge yourself to write your best work, every time; do what you say you're going to do; and do it on deadline.

The challenge is the fun part. If you read back over the last three things you wrote and they all have the same rhythm, you're stuck in a rut. Dare yourself to try something new. Start out with a quote instead of ending with one. Try a new descriptive technique. Circle around and end with a reference to something you mentioned at the very start. Make yourself a better writer, constantly.

I think editors are pretty easy to please. They simply expect you to deliver what you promised, without a lot of hand-holding (on their parts) and hand-wringing (on yours). If you propose a storyline to an editor and then, in the course of interviewing, you find out the story is going to differ significantly, tell the editor right away. And look for artistic and photographic possibilities to illustrate your story while you're researching and interviewing. Give those ideas (with contact information) to the editor. You're adding value to what you sell. Every client likes a little icing on the cake.◆

9.

Journalistically Speaking

Think about it: How many rubber-chicken lunches in hotel ballrooms have you been to in your career? Hundreds? Aside from memories of damage done to your digestive system, you might recall that the speakers frequently are authors who have written about the topic at hand. Whether they're book authors or journalists, they know a great deal about their subject, and their speeches are often peppered with personal anecdotes about their experiences while researching or writing about their topic.

Don't be surprised if after you've published an article about, for example, cost accounting for the masses, somebody from the National Association of Cost Accountants contacts you and asks you to speak at the group's local convention.

Speaking and teaching engagements have become natural outgrowths of a writing career. These engagements can serve a variety of purposes. Speaking engagements can help boost your career by exposing you to a lot of people all at once and letting them know what you specialize in and how you present your topic. You can use teaching to stabilize your income, because you'll receive a regular check every month. Your value to an editor increases when you are out in the field, talking to business people about their concerns. By speaking and teaching, you will make valuable contacts that will give you ideas for stories, a wealth of contacts for interviews, and exposure to business trends and hot-button issues.

In this chapter, we'll show you how to use your writing expertise and knowledge of your topic to develop career-enhancing speaking and teaching gigs.

Speak to Me

Why do writers become speakers and how does that happen? As you've already learned, writers research topics, gather a body of knowledge on those topics, and then use a mere fraction of it for the actual printed story. The rest of the knowledge sits in a file cabinet and pollutes the writer's brain with seemingly useless information. The more you work at your niche, the more you'll collect information on it, and the more information you collect, the closer you are to becoming an expert who can speak knowledgeably about your subject.

When Emily worked at *Natural Foods Merchandiser*, she wrote and edited a section of the magazine specifically about the business of selling natural foods. Every year, at the industry's annual convention, the trade-show organizers asked her to speak about the economy and the natural foods business. This was a very popular session, and it often attracted several hundred people.

Emily's byline had been associated over and over again with coverage of the business side of organic and natural foods. Although she wasn't an economist, or a natural foods retailer, she knew enough about the topic from talking to sources and developing her body of knowledge.

It was also a very exciting time to be speaking about changes in the natural foods industry. The industry at first consisted of small businesses run by individuals and families. Then, many natural foods companies caught IPO fever: six or seven did initial public offerings and became publicly traded. Emily's confidence in her knowledge of this industry trend overcame her inexperience at speaking. By watching other speakers, and noting how they organized their speeches into entertaining, funny, and informative talks, she evolved into a speaker, too.

As editor of *New Mexico Business Weekly*, Emily is frequently asked to give speeches about various topics, ranging from "how to get press coverage" to "the state of the New Mexico economy." She has spoken to chamber of commerce groups, engineering societies, marketing professionals, and public-relations groups. She has had no training in public speaking, save for a brief course during her MBA program, and her experience in business, giving presentations, and running meetings.

If you've developed the expert knowledge it takes to write about something, why not turn that knowledge into a little extra money? In chapter 2, we talked about expert columnists. Your writing, in some cases, makes you an expert, whether it's on your chosen beat or niche, or on writing and publishing itself. Expert columnists are most frequently asked to speak about their topic.

Let's return for a moment to Jeffrey Gitomer, the columnist we mentioned in chapter 4, "Turn Your Contacts into Great Interviews." As a sales consultant, he spends most of his time giving workshops and speeches. Most of those speaking engagements are generated from his weekly column, which runs in business newspapers from coast to coast. Gitomer has a strong voice and an anecdotal style, and his speeches are highly entertaining: the topics he speaks about feed his columns, and his columns feed his speeches.

Speaking of Writing

Browse through the speakers list of any writers' conference, and you're sure to find a whole roster of working writers giving speeches on topics that range from tips for cracking the magazine business to writing the personality profile.

Your name, too, could be on that roster. The most obvious speaking engagement for the freelance or staff writer is the anecdotal, "how I did it" speech. Nearly everyone is interested in stories, and stories make the best speeches. As you progress in your writing career, you'll make mistakes, you'll learn secret tips that work for you, you'll develop your own tricks of the trade. Just as if you were writing an article, the best speeches will come from expounding upon a single, tightly focused angle.

So once again, we advise you to keep a folder. Every time you come across a particular problem, write it on a slip of paper and store it in the folder. Hopefully, you'll also come across the solution, and store that, too. The crazier the mishap, the funnier it will be to tell later as an anecdote. From the banal to the ridiculous, from the tragic to the career-busting, people want to hear about it.

As you keep your anecdotes, also keep a list of organizations that might be interested in your spiel. Meeting planners may call you right from the start of your speaking career. But if that doesn't happen fast enough, you may want to spend some time networking. When you go to writers' conferences, introduce yourself to the organizers, tell them what you'd like to speak about, and then follow up.

If you belong to professional organizations, be aware that many of them have speakers' bureaus that offer experts on many subjects to local groups. Get on the list.

Speak What You Know

Now an important word about how to make your speeches just as special as your writing: develop an angle to your speaking pitch, just as you develop a strong angle for your writing. Don't just sell yourself as a successful writer—there are plenty of successful writers. Offer the audience something more. For example, you could develop a speech on "ten freelance writing mistakes I made, and how you can avoid them." Now you've got a strong topic and a natural outline that includes all of your speaking points.

Just as you write in more than one niche or subspecialty, you can speak on a variety of topics. If you read biographies of writers who speak about writing, for example, you'll notice they've got a whole list of topics they'll offer the audience: "Five freelance markets you've never considered"; "When I was young: five memoir writing techniques"; "Seven ways to waste your writing time." Note that these examples contain numbered lists. This is a tried and true speaking (and writing) technique that can greatly help novice speechmakers develop and frame effective speeches. Draw up a list of strong writing-related topics, with clever angles and titles, then get networking.

You can also cross-market yourself as an expert on your beat or niche. Many experts began their careers as writers and have turned that niche into a career speaking and teaching on the topic. If you get involved deeply in a beat, over time you'll know a lot more than the average person working in the industry. You'll be two steps ahead when it comes to trends, and you'll have interviewed all the experts. That's when you can leverage that knowledge into speaking engagements. In Emily's job as editor of *New Mexico Business Weekly*, she's frequently asked to comment on the state of the New Mexico economy, both for TV news and in speeches. Although she's no economist, she can speak intelligently on the topic because she looks at the quarterly economic statistics, tracks all kinds of businesses and industries, and can view the trends over time.

As you become acquainted with the movers and shakers in your niche, you'll undoubtedly have some contact with the professional associations related to that industry. Often, your first speaking engagement will originate with one of these local groups.

Be advised that these local groups may not pay. Most writers who want to transition to speaking, or add that to their repertoire of skills, begin by taking unpaid gigs. The point is to build a reputation, to have people see your style and to practice. Later, you can sign up with a speakers' bureau and command a fee (see our sidebar interview with Elaine Dundon in this chapter).

But be forewarned: not all writers are great speakers. Speaking is like acting. You have to be able to hold an audience's attention, gauge its reaction to your current speech, and modify it on the fly if you feel their attention wandering. You have to be entertaining and offer information to the audience in a unique and humorous way. This takes practice and experience. Start small, speaking to smaller groups (which are sometimes more challenging than large ones because of the intimacy between speaker and audience), develop various styles and tones that you can modify as you become more experienced. You may want to see a professional coach and have yourself videotaped.

Why You Are Already a Teacher

Think about the best teachers you've ever had. They were undoubtedly lifelong learners who gained great joy from learning and passing that knowledge on to others. They were clear and insightful. They were passionate about their subject and engaged the classroom with personal experience, anecdotes, and humor.

As a writer, you're a natural learner: every time you write an article, you learn something new. That's why writing is a great profession for the lifelong student or teacher. When you research and write an article, you're learning something new about your topic, and you're informing your audience clearly, and with a certain style. Not only that, but you've learned how to become a successful writer. That topic alone could keep you busy speaking to writing groups, teaching a class in the adult education program of your local college or university, or coaching other writers individually or in groups.

When someone reads your magazine or newspaper articles, they do so to be entertained, but in the process they learn something new. Your readers search your articles for tips, advice, or because the topics interest them and they want to learn more. You are teaching them something they didn't know.

You may be surprised to find your expertise in a given subject desirable. Don't be: throughout your writing career, you'll develop a depth of knowledge even scholars would envy. You've interviewed the industry's pundits, you've met its players, you are well known among the community in your beat. You may be called upon to speak about or teach a topic within your beat, or you may be called upon to teach a writing class. It's all part of the organic growth of your career, and it may come to you without your active pursuit of it.

> **Five Reasons You're Already A Good Teacher**
>
> 1. You've run plenty of meetings in your profession. Managing a classroom is exactly like running a meeting, except you dictate the agenda and the to-do list.
> 2. You've given speeches and prepared reports.
> 3. You have oodles of real-world experience. This makes for an exciting, relevant, and fun classroom.
> 4. You're a lifelong learner. Otherwise you wouldn't be pursuing a writing career.
> 5. You know how to organize your thoughts into a coherent, interesting presentation.

Get Started Speaking and Teaching

To develop your speaking and teaching career, begin with local chapters of trade associations. If you write about retailing, you may want to contact the local retail association and ask to speak at an upcoming association luncheon on a unique topic you've covered or a trend you've noticed.

Think of the outgrowths of retailing, too, and contact those related associations. The American Marketing Association, for example, has chapters in each city and has monthly luncheons. You could spin your retail topic for marketing, advertising, purchasing, or a general "state of the economy" speech. Just as in your writing, you can take one topic and develop five different speeches from it.

Many chambers of commerce have after-work networking programs that address different topics. Generally there's a speaker followed by a cocktail hour, or vice versa. Get in touch with the program manager for your local chamber or ones in surrounding areas, and let he or she know you're available to speak on your topic at the organization's next mixer.

It's always a good idea to get in touch with speakers' bureaus. Some have very strict requirements, others are more lax. You'll need to have a strong list of topics, and you'll need to have a sample video of your presentation. Browse speakers' bureau websites to get an idea of what kinds of speakers they use and how to sign up.

Many writers supplement their income with a steady teaching job. It can provide regular income and interaction with other people—something writers need periodically. Community colleges or the adult education programs of the local university nearly always offer some kind of journalism or writing program. Check out the catalog over the course of time and see what kinds of classes they offer. Is there something missing you could suggest? Perhaps the same person has been teaching the same course for several years. You might suggest a fresh angle on the same old thing. If you've already spoken publicly, include those engagements on the résumé you prepare for the school. It will help your credibility and allow you to sell yourself as someone capable of managing a classroom.

And don't forget to include your writing clips. For journalism and adult education, most colleges and universities are looking for practitioners—people who've been through the process and can advise students on how it's done. Real-world experience counts here more than a passel of letters after your name.

Teaching is the ultimate job for a writer to have. It allows plenty of time off to work on projects (long summer and winter breaks), it stimulates the brain, and it provides a steady (if not terribly large) paycheck. And usually one teaching job leads to another. Over the years, Emily has taught writing in Summit County and Denver, Colorado; Haverhill, Massachusetts; and at the University of New Mexico in Albuquerque. She sought out her first teaching job during a slow period in her freelance career, and maintained it through several semesters, even after she'd been hired as a full-time writer. The rest of the jobs came easily—experience and good references landed her the position at Northern Essex Community College in Haverhill. That school was specifically looking for someone with real-world experience.

Your skills as a teacher and a speaker are already well developed. Because you understand your field, and are a professional, you already have the skills for the job. You have run meetings, given presentations, and developed teams that worked successfully together. That's all teaching is—running a meeting where you get to decide the agenda and the to-do list over the course of a semester. And because you've studied the field, you know what the students need to learn. You just need to organize your thoughts.

To Do Today

Getting the Gig

- ☐ Contact your local chapter of your professional association. Ask how you can get on the speakers list. Don't expect to be paid the first time out.
- ☐ Find out who's organizing the national association meeting and where it is. Ask if they'd consider letting you moderate a panel session—this requires introducing the speakers and asking provocative questions during the question-and-answer session. It's a great way to make yourself known as a future speaker.
- ☐ Join Toastmasters, or take a presentations course at a local business school (most now require their MBA students to take such a class).
- ☐ Watch great speakers, and take notes. How do they pace themselves? How do they use humor or visual aids? How much information do they present and how so they present it? How do they interact with the audience?

Teaching

- ☐ Gather the course catalogs for local colleges and universities. Don't forget to check into the adult-education catalogs.
- ☐ Find out what classes are offered and which ones aren't. What semesters seem to have holes?
- ☐ Write a list of classes you could teach. Give them a few titles, like "Five ways to streamline your manufacturing operation," and write up a paragraph description for each one.
- ☐ Contact the dean or department head. Set up an informational interview. Ask how you get on the adjunct faculty list. What's the procedure?

- ☐ Do an Internet search of syllabi for your potential textbooks and structure. If you type "magazine writing classes" in a search engine, you'll be able to see what other professors have done with the topic. Pull out the best ideas that suit your style and develop an outline. Have this organized when you go in for your informational interview.
- ☐ Be prepared to teach a fake class. Often colleges will ask a prospective teacher to give a class to other teachers before it'll hire them. Don't be intimidated. Just pretend you're with students. Make sure you explain things slowly and clearly, don't cover too much in one class, and use visual aids if you can.

Interview with Elaine Dundon,

MBA, the founder of The Innovation Group Consulting Inc. (www.innovationguru.com). She is a speaker, trainer, consultant, and the author of the best-selling book *The Seeds of Innovation*, and co-author of *The Innovative Organization Assessment: A Holistic Approach*.

What are the advantages of speaking engagements in terms of growing my professional writing career?

The net advantage of my speaking engagements is to promote my work in the area of innovative thinking and to further enhance my positioning as an expert in this area. Speaking to new audiences helps me share my unique approach, which, in turn, leads to increased interest in my training services and for my book[s].

What's the best way to land a speaking engagement?

In my experience, the best way is to connect with a speakers bureau which, in turn, will connect you with potential clients for speaking engagements. I have an exclusive arrangement with the National Speakers Bureau for the Canadian marketplace but work on a project-by-project basis with speakers bureaus in the United States.

It is also important to have content. In other words, to be able to offer an educated perspective (lots of examples, concepts, etc.) in your specific area. A client wants to know that you are a credible source of information in addition to being an inspirational speaker. Having been an adjunct professor at the university level, in my specialty of innovation management, has lead to speaking engagements, as well as [having] served to enhance my credibility in this area.

Once you have a few speaking engagements under your belt, it is easier to land future speaking engagements since you now have a list of references and feedback to share with prospective clients.

What skills do you possess that also make you a great choice as a speaker?

You must have content-specialized knowledge and experience and the ability to hold the audience's interest as well as inspire them. In addition, you have to have the ability to organize thoughts and present them in a coherent and engaging manner. I have the ability to adapt my message to suit specific objectives. Also you must be professional—I know how to present myself professionally and to work with the client to make sure their event is successful.

Did you receive any professional coaching? What new skills did you need to develop?

I recommend that anyone who transitions from being a writer to a speaker, or vice versa, invest the time and effort to receive some coaching from others who are more experienced. In my case, I developed (and am still developing) my speaking skills through lots of experience teaching at the university level, speaking to different audiences of different backgrounds and sizes (100 to 1,500 participants), asking for feedback from my speakers bureau, asking all clients for feedback following a speaking or training session and asking other experienced speakers for guidance. My partner, Alex Pattakos, who is a dynamic and passionate speaker, has provided very valuable feedback and coaching.◆

10.

Writers Are People Who Write

Years ago, Emily took a magazine-writing class at the University of Colorado in Boulder. One of the students asked, "How do I become a writer?" The teacher, a well-published magazine writer, simply said, "Writers are people who write."

You are a writer now. We hope you have had some publishing success using the advice in this book, that you are writing regularly and enjoying the process. Whether you write about specific aspects of, or trends in, your industry, or supplement your income or pension with article writing, or have moved onto writing as a full-time pursuit, we congratulate you.

Many handbooks on writing tell you that you must write every day, seven days a week, on assignment or just in a personal journal, to keep your skills honed. We don't feel that way. You have a job and written communication is part of that job, whether you're writing a client presentation or filling out a form. If you are also writing articles, even part time, you're getting plenty of practice. A good deal of your time, perhaps one-third, perhaps half, will be taken up with other tasks that are part of the business of writing—research, interviews, marketing, networking, and correspondence.

It is true, however, that the less you do something, the less you feel like doing it. As with any craft, practice makes you better, and to practice you must write.

You may not always be in the midst of an assignment. In fact, those less-busy days represent quality time in which you can sit down with pen and paper and let it flow. Just let the words come; don't worry about grammar, sentence structure, or style. Your assignment is to free some creative juice.

This free-writing exercise is also a great way to start working on an assignment. If you find your writing tight or blocked, just riff for fifteen or twenty minutes. Set a timer and sit down at the computer, or with a pad and pen, and write down whatever comes into your head. Don't stop until your timer rings. Then get up, stretch, pour yourself a cup of coffee, and open a document. The writing will come easier.

Writing is not all joyous creation. Like much of what you do for a living, writing is detailed, time-consuming work that can be grueling. Under stress, bad work habits that you didn't know you had suddenly appear out of nowhere to derail your efforts. We've experienced them all and we hope, in this chapter, to help you keep them at bay.

Think of this chapter as the customer-service segment of our book. As a writer, you are on the frontlines every day, putting your-

How to Meet Your Deadlines Every Time

1. Count backwards from the due date of your article so you know how much time you have to complete it.
2. Estimate the time it takes you to do each task—research, writing questions, interviewing, transcribing tapes and notes, writing, and redrafting, if necessary. Your best guess is all that is needed for this step.
3. Add it up. Count backwards from the deadline date, as if you had nothing else to do but write this article. This exercise will give you the last possible date on which you can begin working on it.
4. Mark that date on your calendar. If the subject of the assignment is more difficult, or if you have more than one assignment due within the same time period, move the date even farther away from the deadline to allow yourself more time.
5. Leave yourself additional time in which to be flexible. You may be surprised at how far in advance your starting date is.

self out there in person and in words, to your editors and your readers. They are your public, and they are your clients. As such, they expect certain behaviors and courtesies, just as clients do in your present industry. A professional writer is expected to produce work on time and to word count. You will be expected to comport yourself professionally in your dress and demeanor—after all, you represent the publication to its public, whether you are on staff or a freelance writer. Your answering machine will have a professional, informative message. As in any other business, you will observe the basics of doing business.

We hope to help you polish your image as a published professional. Here, we give you our best advice on how to avoid the pitfalls that mark other writers as rookies, and to adopt good writing practices that will help your work, and you, shine.

Good Work Habits Support Good Writing

Face Down Procrastination

Many writers waste time. In fact, on most writers' business cards it should say: Writer, Procrastinator. Even as we write these sentences, the dog brings his toy over and wants to play, a slice of chocolate cake in the refrigerator is calling out to us, the dishes beg to be done. There are a million distractions to keep us from writing. But that's all they are: distractions. We're afraid to sit down and face that blank page. We invent reasons for this fear, like "the creative process" and "writer's block." When we simply sit down and put one word after another on the page, however, the fear fades and the flow takes over.

Some people say they work better under pressure. We don't buy that. Although the creative juices may flow more freely because you're down to the deadline, we doubt the result will be your best work.

Like a good loaf of bread, writing needs to rest. The writer needs time to look at the article with a fresh eye, an eye that has not been tweaking and reworking and adding for the past twelve hours and twelve cups of coffee. If you let a story rest for two days, or even a week (you can afford the time if you don't procrastinate), you will see paragraphs in the story that must be moved, sentences that don't quite say what they should, pieces of your research that are not relevant to the story. You'll be able to find superfluous phrases, and other places where you can cut the fat.

Give yourself time to turn in a piece that is truly finished. Like a loaf of bread, work it, let it rest, and work it again. Make sure the structure is tight, the facts are complete, and the storyline has no holes. Be certain that the writing is clean, interesting, and cliché-free, and the grammar, flawless. Ask the editor which style guide the publication uses—*The Associated Press Stylebook and Briefing on Media Law*, for example, or *The Chicago Manual of Style* (see "Suggested Reading," pages 125–6)—and be sure you are adhering to its rules. Check that the manuscript is precisely the right length and configured in the way your editor requires. Get your invoice ready to go. You can't do all of that when you wait until the last minute to get started.

If you need other reasons not to procrastinate, skip to "Never Miss a Deadline" (page 117).

Follow Instructions

Write down everything the editor says during that initial conversation—the one where he or she tells you exactly which angle to take on the story, whom to interview, and how many words to write. Offer your opinions about the angle; however, remember that the editor is your customer and you are providing the product that he or she wants to buy.

Keep those editorial notes posted near your computer, and every single time you sit down to work on the piece, review them (or the assignment letter or contract, in a more formal work-for-hire arrangement). This practice will help you stay on track, and warn you if you start to stray from the original assignment.

When you've finished the story, look over the notes again. Did you deliver what the editor wanted? Or did you veer off? If you did, is there a reason for it? Were you unable to get a key interview, or did you miss a piece of information in the research? Did the story you followed evolve into a different, more accurate, or more interesting angle?

Journalistic objectivity requires that you follow a story where it leads. However, if you were about to ship a product to a customer that was substantially different from what the customer ordered, you'd call first to tell the customer why the substitute product was a better deal. As soon as you know that the terms have changed, call the editor before you file a story that differs substantially from the original assignment.

Keep in Touch

Unless you've got a well-developed and trusting relationship with an editor, it's a great idea to check in every once in a while. For example, if you have six weeks to work on a story, call every couple of weeks and give your editor an update. This will give him or her a good idea of your work ethic, how the piece is coming along, and whether the piece is staying on point and on assignment (see "Follow Instructions," page 116). That way, if you run into problems, you can immediately seek your editor's advice and assistance.

If you think you might miss a deadline, call immediately and give the editor a heads-up. In our experience with editors, you get one "family emergency" per career.

Never Miss a Deadline

Never do it. Ever. Period.

Your assignment, whether it was formalized with a handshake or a contract, is your word. Pros don't go back on their word. The writers that reap repeat assignments do what they say they are going to do—on point, to word count, and on time. Editors love these writers. Be one of them.

Writers who miss deadlines are considered amateurs by editors and by other writers. Missing a deadline throws off the rhythm of a publication, which must chug along relentlessly toward its own deadlines. If you are late turning in an assignment, you affect the schedules of editorial, production, and distribution people. Your own work piles up behind you. It may become impossible to meet other deadlines down the road, and so on. Given the choice between a chronically late, but excellent writer and one who hands in finished work on time, which will the editor hire?

Don't Take Editing Personally

Every writer gets edited, without exception. Even if you've think you've written the greatest articles known to humanity, you undoubtedly will have to eat a slice of humble pie some day.

Each publication has its own style and attitude. And every editor will give you a different take on the story. Just listen carefully to what your editor wants, and learn to adapt your style and content to your editor's expectations. Don't argue. The more you work with an editor, the more you'll be in tune with the publication's style, and the more frequently you will turn in stories that your editor loves on the first read.

Editors change jobs frequently. If your favorite editor leaves, make a lunch appointment with the replacement editor. The new editor will have his or her own style; listen carefully to what he or she wants. Ask the editor to point out articles that publication has published in the past that are considered excellent examples of the articles he or she will publish in future.

Never Fudge It, Rearrange It, or Misquote It

We don't mean to impugn your code of ethics here, but every writer is tempted to at least correct an interviewee's grammar every now and then. If your source didn't say it exactly the way you wish they had said it, ask the same question in a different way. If you still can't get what you want, resign yourself to the fact that you may not. But don't, ever, fudge it. You'll be found out, we guarantee it.

Five Things We Will Never Do Again

We also know firsthand that good writers can learn from their mistakes and go on to make their writing and their careers even better. Here are five errors of judgment we have made in our writing and editing careers. We are red-faced as we write them, but are still willing to share them with you as object lessons in how *not* to look like a professional writer.

1. Yell at your source

Most of the hundreds of people we have interviewed over the past fifteen years were courteous, well-spoken experts in their fields. Of course, the few not-so-nice ones stand out in memory.

Stephanie once auditioned for the freelance position of small business how-to writer for a nonprofit organization's monthly newspaper. As she began to explain why she was calling, her first and primary interviewee for the tryout article interrupted and began to yell and curse. Stephanie yelled back (*sans* cursing) and hung up.

Luckily, her next interviewee knew the first, knew that he had a reputation for screaming at people, and that many of his own colleagues avoided talking to him. The second interviewee agreed to speak with Stephanie's editor about the incident, and even suggested a more appropriate expert for the article. Stephanie

> **Promote Your Professional Image**
>
> 1. Be courteous to and respectful of all interviewees.
> 2. Listen to and acknowledge what the editor wants.
> 3. Know the publication's policies.
> 4. Write specifically for your market.
> 5. Insist on being paid in a timely fashion.

wrote the article and got the job, but not without a sleepless night or two over what her own behavior might have cost her.

No matter how much hostility you must tolerate from an interviewee, be polite. If you find yourself sorely tried, remember that the frequency of your writing assignments rests on your reputation. Don't put yourself in a bad light.

2. Don't listen to the editor

Emily's assignment to write an article on safe and happy horse-trailering for an equestrian magazine included two sources to call, both of whom were suggested by the editor.

One source was uncooperative, repeatedly missing interview appointments and not returning her phone calls. So Emily went off looking for other experts. But the editor had especially wanted the unavailable source in the story. She was even willing to extend the deadline by two months to make it happen.

Not only had Emily veered off without first checking with the editor, but she hadn't thought of asking for an extension. The proper way to handle it would have been to call the editor and explain the situation, letting the editor suggest a solution. Once again, we remind you that the editor is your customer, and the customer is always right.

3. Send an article to a source for review before publication

Letting an interviewee read your article before it is published is the editor's prerogative only, and usually it is not done at all. Emily failed to inform an intern who was working for her of this crucial fact of journalism.

The intern was working on a feature-length story about a local vocational school. Although the story seemed fairly noncontroversial, the intern decided to have the source read the story, and faxed it to her. The next day, Emily got an irate call from the source, who claimed the story misrepresented the school, herself, and her quotes. The intern had ruined her relationship with the source. Emily apologized for what she explained was unedited work. She pulled the story and assigned it to another, more experienced reporter.

Interviewees will ask if they can see the article before it is published. It is up to the editor to determine whether or not a prepublication article will be sent to a source for any reason. Know the publication's policy on this matter so you will be able to recite it professionally.

4. Try to sell your work to a publication that doesn't publish what you write

Stephanie received a telephone call from an editor at Simon & Schuster who had seen her work in another publication. The editor wanted Stephanie to write an article on career strategies for nonfamily employees of family-owned corporations.

Having written on family-owned business matters many times, Stephanie turned out an article in which she interviewed an expert psychologist in the subject, and handed it in. The editor rejected the story immediately. All of the articles in this particular publication were written in the style of expert columns—writers well versed in their subjects who spoke as experts themselves. By interviewing an outside expert, Stephanie violated the tone and style of the magazine.

She forgot the basic rule of sales: know your market. Read the publication thoroughly before you try to write for it. See chapter 2, "What the Market Will Bear," for advice on analyzing magazines and newspapers before you write for them.

5. Take assignments from clients who pay on publication

Magazines fail at an astonishing rate. New publications, often undercapitalized, start up every day. Some magazines work on issues from six to eight months in advance. Unless you want to work for nothing, ask to be paid upon acceptance. Acceptance means that you have turned in the entire article and the editor has read and approved it.

Emily once freelanced for an alternative magazine in Boston. Although the business seemed reputable, they moved their offices frequently. Additionally, their payment policy kept changing, until they adjusted it to read "on publication." All signs pointed to a magazine in trouble. At times, it took as long as three months for them to pay her. Emily felt she was in a race to get paid for all of her work before they shut down.

Get the publication's terms in writing, and make sure they know your terms. Make it clear that you are to be paid within fifteen days of acceptance, or fifteen days from the date on your invoice. Type "Net 15" on the bottom of your invoice. Charge interest just like a regular business if they miss a payment. If necessary, send a statement every month to remind them of what they owe you. Craft a concise, polite, but to-the-point collection letter, if it comes to that. But we caution you to negotiate the terms at the outset, especially with a new customer. Don't settle for "payment on publication."

We hope that we have given you enough information, advice and tools to launch a successful business writing career. Remember these words of advice: treat your writing career as you would a business. Develop a strong niche, find customers who will buy your well-designed and useful product, and market yourself using the best practices of the business. We know you will succeed.

To Do Today

- ☐ Set aside some unhurried time for free writing to help you limber up. Think of it as a brain stretch to help you ward off procrastination.
- ☐ Call your editor. Go over your notes on your next story and track how closely you are sticking to the original assignment. If the story is leading you down another path, check in. If it's been a few weeks since the initial assignment, just call and let your editor know how it is going.
- ☐ Find out your publication's official policy on prepublication review by interviewees. Write a script so you know what to tell an interviewee who asks to read the article before it is published.
- ☐ Use our sidebar "How to Meet Your Deadlines Every Time," (page 114) to calculate the time you will need to complete your next assignment.

Interview with Tania Casselle,

a freelance writer since 1995. Casselle has been features editor on a group of international business magazines for the fashion and textiles industries. She also worked as a public-relations and marketing consultant. She writes for publications in the United States, Europe, and Asia.

What's the mark of a professional writer?

They know their market and recognize that their job is to cater to the needs of that market. They understand the readerships of the target publications. Professional journalists treat their writing as a business, not as an art form. They understand that the amount of time spent on writing will be much less than the amount of time spent on researching stories, interviewing sources, marketing themselves, sending out queries, invoicing, accounting, etc. Professional writers also understand the relationship between writer and editor is based on a mutual business benefit. Always go into discussions knowing that you have something to offer, the editor needs writers to fill [his or her] pages, you are presenting your query professionally, and it is a business transaction, not about you personally. Attend business conferences and press events, join professional groups, get yourself out there so people know what you do and what you have to offer.

What are the telltale signs of an inexperienced writer?

Inexperienced writers give themselves away in many ways, but it generally comes down to not understanding the needs of the publications they are trying to sell to and how to go about meeting those needs. Inexperienced writers often make the mistake of submitting a complete written article for consideration, rather than an outline query, which is then discussed with the editor and completed under assignment. And they often take rejection personally if an editor refuses a story idea.

There are only two sane responses to rejection. One is to learn from it, to see why the editor turned the proposal down, why it didn't suit their publication, or what was missing, so next time you can try a different approach. The second sane response is just to turn that query around, reslant it for another publication, and send it out again. It's a numbers game.

What qualities make you desirable as a freelancer? Is it skill? Great story ideas? Timeliness? Writing to word count? How much do the little things count?

Two qualities make a freelance business writer desirable: the confidence to communicate what you know and to admit what you don't know. A good knowledge of the industry sector or business discipline means you can write the piece with subtlety [and] insight, showing the ramifications of the story within a broader context. It also means you have the savvy not to fall for p.r. hype! Where your knowledge has gaps, strong research skills are essential, as is a willingness to admit ignorance where necessary. There's no shame in saying "I don't understand that terminology, or that technology, what does it mean?"

The second quality is an understanding of an editor's needs, then working hard to meet those needs by submitting [quality] copy on deadline, to word count with the piece reworked until it's as good as it can be—always written, of course, with their specific readership in mind.

The details are important. The names must be spelled right and the facts must be as straight as you can get them. The copy must be in on time.

What's the one thing that will endear a writer to an editor? The one thing that will turn off an editor?

Doing what you say you will do, when you say you will do it, will endear a writer to an editor, and more importantly result in repeat assignments!

Not being reliable, either in timeliness or quality of work, will turn editors off. If you get your facts wrong and upset their readers—who in the field of business publications also tend to be their advertisers— editors will receive complaints and will be very unhappy with the writer.◆

Appendix

Suggested Reading List

Books on Journalism

Floating Off the Page: The Best Stories from the Wall Street Journal's *Middle Column*. Ken Wells, editor. New York: The Free Press, 2002.

Kovach, Bill, and Tom Rosenstiel. *The Elements of Journalism: What Newspeople Should Know and the Public Should Expect*. New York: Crown Publishers, 2001.

Stewart, James B. *Follow the Story: How to Write Successful Nonfiction*. New York: Simon & Schuster, 1998.

Books on Getting Published

2004 Writer's Market. Katie Struckel Brogan and Robert Brewer, editors. Cincinnati: Writer's Digest Books, 2004.

Appelbaum, Judith. *How to Get Happily Published*. 5th ed. New York: HarperCollins*Publishers*, 1998.

Emerson, Connie. *The Writer's Guide to Conquering the Magazine Market*. Cincinnati: Writer's Digest Books, 1991.

Money for Writers: Grants, Awards, Prizes, Contests, Scholarships, Retreats, Resources, Conferences, and Internet Information. Diane Billot, editor. New York: Henry Holt and Company, 1997.

Books on Writing Style

The Associated Press Stylebook and Briefing on Media Law. Norm Goldstein, editor. Cambridge: Perseus Publishing, 2002.

Blundell, William E. *The Art and Craft of Feature Writing*. New York: Dow Jones & Company, 1986.

Franklin, Jon. *Writing for Story*. New York: Penguin Group, 1994.

Gutkind, Lee. *The Art of Creative Nonfiction*. New York: John Wiley & Sons, Inc., 1997.

McKinney, Don. *Magazine Writing That Sells*. Cincinnati: Writer's Digest Books, 1994.

Nuwer, Hank. *How to Write Like an Expert about Anything*. Cincinnati: Writer's Digest Books, 1995.

O'Conner, Patricia T. *Words Fail Me: What Everyone Who Writes Should Know about Writing*. New York: Harcourt, 2000.

Strunk, William Jr., et al. *The Elements of Style*. 4th ed. Boston: Allyn & Bacon, 2000.

Zinsser, William K. *On Writing Well: The Classic Guide to Writing Nonfiction*. 25th Anniversary ed. New York: HarperResource, 2001.

Zinsser, William K. *Writing to Learn*. New York: HarperCollins Publishers, 1989.

Books on Grammar

Hale, Constance. *Sin and Syntax: How to Craft Wickedly Effective Prose*. New York: Broadway Books, 1999.

Hacker, Diana. *A Writer's Reference*. 4th ed. New York: Bedford / St. Martin's, 2002.

O'Conner, Patricia T. *Woe Is I: The Grammarphobe's Guide to Better English in Plain English*. New York: Putnam, 1996.

Useful Websites

www.bartleby.com

Quotes, definitions, translations, usage. Literary, medical, and almanac reference guide.

www.poyntner.org

The Poytner Institute's website carries articles, tips, and training to improve your writing. Excellent source of ideas for story angles.

www.notrain-nogain.com

Newspaper and journalism training.

Index

Numbers in italics indicate sidebars.

Authors

Stephanie Hainsfurther is a freelance business journalist with seventeen years of experience. She has published more than six hundred articles in regional and national magazines and newspapers, and in international trade journals in the fields of energy, the environment, commercial real estate, and architecture. Recently, Stephanie became the editor-in-chief of *Albuquerque The Magazine*, a lifestyle monthly.

A garden writer, she is also the author of *Pocket Gardening for Your Outdoor Spaces*, published by Hobby House Press in 2004, and is the Southwest region writer for *Gardening How-To* magazine, with more than 600,000 subscribers in the U.S. and Canada. Her column, "Desert Gardener," ran in *New Mexico House & Home* magazine for two years. Stephanie has a BA in English from St. Joseph College in West Hartford, Connecticut.

Emily Esterson is editor of the *New Mexico Business Weekly*. She has been a business journalist for fifteen years, beginning her career as a contributing writer to *Colorado Business* magazine. She has worked as a reporter for the Boulder *Daily Camera*, *Expansion Management*, and *Consulting Magazine*. She was an associate editor for *Inc.* magazine in Boston prior to joining the *New Mexico Business Weekly* in 1999. Her freelance work has appeared in *Business Week*, *Consultants News*, *The Improper Bostonian, Delicious! Magazine*, and *Dressage Today*. Emily has an MBA from the University of Denver and is currently pursuing a MA in nonfiction. She lives with her husband Scot and sixteen animals of various species on a small farm in the South Valley.